TIM NOAKES · STEPHEN GRANGER
RUNNING YOUR BEST

OXFOR
Cape Tow
1995

OXFORD UNIVERSITY PRESS
Walton Street, Oxford OX2 6DP, United Kingdom
Oxford New York
Athens Bangkok Bombay
Calcutta Cape Town Dar es Salaam Delhi
Florence Hong Kong Istanbul Karachi
Kuala Lumpur Madras Madrid Melbourne
Mexico City Nairobi Paris Singapore
Taipei Tokyo Toronto

and associated companies in
Berlin Ibadan

ISBN: 0 19 570 956 X

First published 1995
Third Impression 1997

Photos on pp. 38, 57, 140, 174, 232, 234 and 235 property of
South African Sports Illustrated; used with permission.
Photo on p. 119 property of Zola Budd-Pieterse;
used with permission.

Editor Helen Moffett
Cover design Jennifer Hoare, New Leaf Design

Published by Oxford University Press Southern Africa,
Harrington House, 37 Barrack Street, Cape Town 8001,
South Africa

Typeset by RHT desktop publishing and Baseline
Printed by Clysons

CONTENTS

PREFACE

The cover page of the instruction manual of a recently purchased computer printer urgently warned the reader: 'Before operating this unit, please read these instructions completely.' As the manual ran to well over a hundred pages, mostly written in technical jargon, this was a rather intimidating command to the eager new owner, whose immediate need was to print a straightforward, one-page letter for urgent posting. All the information necessary to 'get started' and perform this task could have been provided by three pages of straightforward text.

We do not want this book to make the same mistake. If you are reading it as a first-time or would-be runner, do not feel you have to scrutinize all the why's and wherefore's of the physiological and mental aspects of running, and memorize the 21 Principles for Running Your Best before you run around the block! We suggest that you first turn to Appendix 2 (p. 211) in order to 'get started' immediately.

If, on the other hand, you are a relatively experienced or competitive runner, we suggest that you study the contents page or simply flip through the book until you find the topic most relevant to your needs.

While coaches and athletes will argue the merits of one specific training schedule over another, we believe that training and racing principles, which form the basis for a successful and satisfying running career, are more important to your success as a runner than specific details of how far and fast you should run on a given day.

The great Australian runner, Herb Elliott, who was unbeaten in the mile or 1 500 m as a senior athlete said: 'The more I speak to athletes, the more convinced I become that the method of training is relatively unimportant. There are many ways to the top . . . the important thing is the attitude of the athlete, the desire to get to the top.'

While we recognise the importance of finding a training programme which suits your particular needs – and we have
included detailed programmes (see Appendix 2, pp. 215 -
227) – our emphasis is on the correct approach to training.
By recognizing your physiological limitations, optimizing your
physical and mental resources, and avoiding training pitfalls,
you will be able to build a framework for a training programme which will enable you to run your best. Good luck –
and remember to enjoy yourselves!

I

WHAT DETERMINES ATHLETIC PERFORMANCE?

1 WHAT DETERMINES PERFORMANCE?

Physiological factors

It is unfortunate that the most important factor preventing our achieving running greatness, our genetic make-up, is the one about which we can do very little. It is our choice of parents, more than anything else, which determines whether we will join the vast majority of runners able to complete a standard marathon in three to four hours, or a more elite selection able to complete the marathon in just over two hours. Try as we may, if our genes have destined us to be back-of-the-pack 'hackers', this is where we will remain. Fortunately, the pleasure derived from our chosen sport of running is not solely dependent on our attaining world-beating standards. For those whose genetic gifts have enabled them to attempt such heights, this will always be a motivating factor. But for others like ourselves, there will always be the satisfaction of exploring the limits of our ability, of simply running our best.

Even if our genetic make-up precludes us from ever winning an Olympic gold medal, or even just a local marathon or fun run, we need not despair. There are several other factors to be investigated which can improve our performance and uncover otherwise untapped ability. However, before we focus on these factors in Chapters 2 and 3, we need to understand those physiological limitations which provide the framework within which we can improve performance. These factors include the maximum capacity of the body to do work for short periods of time (usually 5 to 8 minutes) – often referred to as the maximum oxygen consumption (VO_2 max) – muscle power, resistance to fatigue, running efficiency, running style, response to heat and cold, age and gender, other hereditary traits controlling trainability (our ability to adapt to training) and nutritional factors.

MAXIMUM OXYGEN CONSUMPTION (VO_2 max)

Most runners, at some time or another, have wondered how fast and how far they might run if trained to the maximum. Although we have suggested that there are many factors determining this, part of the answer to these questions can be found in each athlete's ability to transport oxygen in the blood, and pump it to the muscles where it is utilized.

During exercise, the oxygen requirements of the active muscles can be increased virtually instantaneously by as much as twenty-fold. The extent to which the body can increase its use of oxygen will determine, in part, how far and fast the athlete can run.

As far back as the 1920s, it was known that the oxygen consumption of the body increases in direct proportion to running speed. It is generally believed that shortly before you reach your maximum work capacity, or running speed, your rate of oxygen consumption reaches a plateau and does not increase further. Although able to exercise a little harder, the body does not take up any more oxygen. At this point, the maximum oxygen consumption (VO_2 max) has been reached. 'V' is scientific shorthand for the rate of oxygen flow. Thus, VO_2 max is the maximum rate of oxygen flow and is usually expressed relative to body weight.

VO_2 max has been the basis for predicting running ability for many years. However, the failure of VO_2 max to accurately and consistently predict the racing times of all athletes has led to the belief that other factors must play a role. In fact, some recent studies question whether the 'plateau phenomenon' exists at all. These studies suggest that factors unrelated to oxygen consumption by the muscles limit exercise performance. This has focused attention on muscle itself (rather than the heart and circulation) as the factor determining exercise performance, especially when it is prolonged. Thus it is argued that the best athletes are those who have the 'best' muscles; i.e., those able to exercise for the longest periods at the highest running intensities or speeds.

However, given the relationship between oxygen consumption and running speed, those athletes who have the ability to maintain the fastest running speeds for prolonged periods of time will also have higher VO_2 max values than less gifted athletes, who are unable to exercise at such high intensities. It is thus argued that the high VO_2 max values of superior athletes results from muscle factors which allow the athlete to run at high speeds. In other words, the high VO_2

max is not the cause of the athlete's superior running ability; rather, as yet unidentified factors in skeletal muscle allow those muscles to continue contracting at high running speeds, and enable them to better resist the onset of fatigue. The achievement of these high running speeds causes a high rate of oxygen consumption.

The highest reported VO_2 max values in male runners (83 and 85 ml of oxygen measured per kg of body weight per minute, expressed as 83 and 85 ml O_2 kg-1 min-1) have been measured in Dave Bedford, the British athlete who set a world 10 000 m record in 1973, and in Said Aouita, the Moroccan one-time holder of multiple world records, including those for 1 500 m and 5 000 m. The highest value for a female runner was 77 ml O_2 kg-1 min-1. Former world cross-country and marathon champion, Grete Waitz, had a VO_2 max of 73 ml O_2 kg-1 min-1 at her peak. By contrast, VO_2 max values measured in healthy young athletes with mean average ability are much lower, usually between 45 and 55 ml O_2 kg-1 min-1; i.e. about 60% lower than in elite athletes.

MUSCLE POWER AND RESISTANCE TO FATIGUE

The best athletes have muscles with a superior capacity to produce power (superior contractility), measured as a high running speed over short distances, as well as a superior capacity to resist the onset of fatigue (fatigue resistance).

A recent study of the best South African middle- (800 – 3 000 m) and long-distance (5 000 m – 42,2 km) runners shows that the speeds both groups achieved over short distances (1 – 3 km) were quite similar; the middle-distance runners were slightly, but not significantly faster. However, when the distances were increased beyond 5 km, the long-distance runners were able to sustain a significantly and increasingly higher running intensity, expressed as a percentage of VO_2 max. This translated into a higher running speed, and faster finishing times in all races over 5 km. The result was that the long-distance runners were more than five

Johan Fourie, one of the athletes tested at the UCT sports science laboratories, dominated South African middle-distance track running in the 1980s. He still holds the national records for the mile, 2 000 m and 3 000 m

minutes faster over 21.1 km than the middle-distance runners. We now know that if the two groups had been tested over shorter distances (200 – 1000 m), the middle-distance group would probably have been significantly faster than the long-distance group.

Of interest is that the VO_2 max values of the two groups were the same or similar; these values could thus not predict the superior performance of the long-distance runners in races of more than 5 km, confirming that a superior capacity to transport oxygen is by itself not the sole factor determining endurance capacity.

Instead, the factor differentiating the performance of the two groups was the superior 'fatigue resistance' of the long-distance runners, which allowed them to sustain a higher percentage of VO_2 max, and thus higher running speeds in races of more than 5 km. This more than offset any inferiority in muscle contractility relative to the middle-distance group. It would seem that the superior fatigue resistance of the muscles of long-distance runners is not due to any difference in the capacity of their muscles to use oxygen. The similar VO_2 max values of both groups supports this conclusion. Thus, the conventional explanation of higher VO_2 max values does not account for the superior running performance of the long-distance runners.

Thus we conclude that a muscle factor independent of oxygen delivery to, or use by, the muscles explains the superior fatigue resistance of elite long-distance runners. The exact nature of this factor is currently not known, but is the subject of continuing research at our sports science laboratory at the University of Cape Town.

One interesting feature of this study was that all the long-distance runners in this study were black South Africans, whereas all the middle-distance runners were white. We therefore speculate that this superior fatigue resistance is perhaps an (East and South) African attribute. This might help to explain the domination of international distance running by East and South African distance runners, particularly Kenyan athletes.

Although the best athletes have superior muscle contractility as well as superior fatigue resistance, we suggest that these two components of muscle function, which are necessary for superior athletic performance, may not necessarily function equally efficiently in an individual. The ability of the muscle to produce a high power output, measured

as running speed over a short distance (say 200 – 1 000 m), will not by itself produce superior distance runners. Muscles with superior fatigue resistance are the second and essential characteristic. This allows the powerful muscles to continue to produce a high power output for a prolonged period without becoming tired.

The result is that the fastest 1 km runner will also be the fastest over longer distances only if he or she also has muscles with very high fatigue resistance. Alternatively, a runner with less powerful muscles and therefore slower times over 200 – 1 000 m, might still be an exceptional distance runner if he or she is blessed with muscles that have a high degree of fatigue resistance.

Bruce Fordyce is an excellent example of a runner with a very high level of fatigue resistance; his best speeds at distances from 10 – 90 km show only a small reduction with increasing distance. When we discussed the research finding that the running time over 10 km seemed to be the best predictor of 42 and 90 km racing times, Bruce cautioned us that he did not think this was the complete answer. He pointed out, for example, that there were many fast 10 km runners in the Comrades who were faster than himself at all

Mathews Temane, one of South Africa's finest distance athletes (also tested at UCT), reached his peak before South Africa's international isolation ended. In 1987, he set a world best of 60:11 for the half-marathon. Here he is seen celebrating a championship victory with co-winner, Colleen de Reuck

distances up to 60 km. He also thought that a very fast marathon time (less than 2:10, for example), was no guarantee of victory in the Comrades Marathon.

Time has tended to support Bruce's viewpoints. The Comrades has now been completed by two of the world's fastest marathon runners, Willie Mtolo in 1989 and Alberto Salazar in 1994. Yet neither came close to Bruce's phenomenal records. The difference, no doubt, is that although Mtolo and Salazar are more powerful in terms of their ability to run faster over short distances of up to 1 km, Bruce's muscles must possess an extraordinary degree of fatigue resistance, found in very few of the world's great runners. This exceptional fatigue resistance has enabled Bruce to set Comrades records that no runner has yet even approached.

Fatigue resistance is probably the factor that changes most with training. A method for measuring your own fatigue resistance is provided below.

RUNNING EFFICIENCY
(oxygen consumption at any running speed)

The internal combustion engine provides a good illustration of the concept of fuel efficiency. High fuel cost and environmental concern over non-renewable fuel resources have placed a premium on engines with greater fuel economy. Running efficiency is similar, although we are considering the efficient use of oxygen by the human body, rather than petrol by the combustion engine. Running efficiency or economy relates to the oxygen cost of running, or the amount of oxygen required to run at a constant (submaximal) speed.

It is generally found that the best distance runners are also the most economical; i.e., they use less oxygen than other runners when running at the same speed. Because of this oxygen economy, they will also use less fuel (carbohydrate, fat and protein) when running. In events lasting more than about 90 minutes, and in which performance may be limited by a depletion of body fuel reserves (see Chapter 8), this slower rate of fuel use may aid performance.

It is interesting to note that running efficiency may change during different types of exercise; for example, during uphill as opposed to downhill running. So it is possible that runners who are efficient on the flat, may be inefficient while running either up- or downhill. Alternatively, an efficient runner may be less efficient at another activity, such as cycling, than a less able runner. At present, it seems that training is the only factor which improves running efficiency. However, there are probably limits to how much efficiency can be improved.

Predicting running performance

If your peak running speed and your fatigue resistance are known, it then becomes possible to predict your running speed, and thus your finishing time in any long-distance running race.

Researchers from the University of Montreal, Canada have produced a table (Table 1.1) that allows you to calculate your fatigue resistance, and so predict your performance in long-distance races on the basis of your running performance at shorter distances.

To use Table 1.1, you must record times for two of your running distances on the table. These two distances should preferably be at shorter distances separated by about 10 km, say 5 and 15 km, or 10 and 20 km. You then place a ruler connecting the times for the two different races and read off equivalent performance times at other racing distances along the edge of the ruler. Estimated VO_2 max is read off the VO_2 max column; the VO_2 max is the value which corresponds to the predicted 3 km time. Hence a predicted 3 km time of 7:58 corresponds to a VO_2 max of 80 ml O_2/kg/min, whereas a 3 km time of 15:45 corresponds to a VO_2 max of 45 ml O_2/kg/min – the average value for a young male runner.

To calculate your fatigue resistance, the points where the ruler crosses line A (extreme left-hand column on the table) and line B (extreme right-hand column on the table) are noted. Subtracting the value in column B from that in column A gives a value for your fatigue resistance on a scale of -100 to +100. (In theory, fatigue resistance can be rated as high as +300; in practice, a value of +100 corresponds to a horizontal line joining performances at 3 and 42.2 km and is equivalent to the performances of the world's best athletes.)

For example, Said Aouita, the exceptional Moroccan runner, has a fatigue resistance rating of +98, calculated from Table 1.1 on the basis of his 3 km and 5 km times. Similarly, Bruce Fordyce's best 10 km and 42.2 km times of 29:53 and 2:17 give him a fatigue resistance rating of +90, one of the highest values possible. Frith van der Merwe with best 10, 15,

Table 1.1
The Mercier/Leger/Desjardins Nomogram for predicting running performance

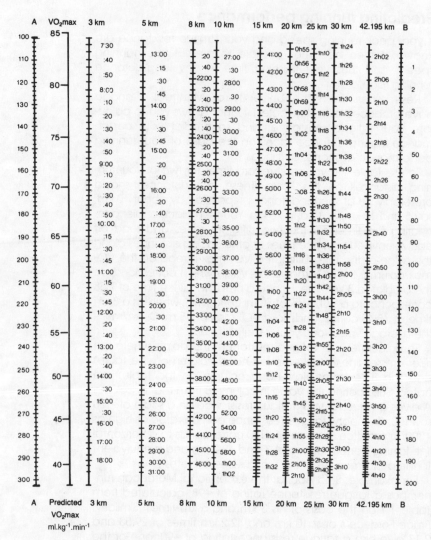

Frith van der Merwe's ultra-distance feats have made South African athletics history; her Comrades and Two Oceans records have yet to be broken. Her extraordinary fatigue resistance gives a clue as to what made her achieve-ments possible. Here she races to a national marathon record of 2:27:36 at Port Elizabeth

21 and 42.2 km times of 33:19, 49:44, 1:11:42 and 2:27:36 shows a remarkable fatigue resistance of +110 (using her 10 km and 21 km or her 15 km and 42 km times); enough to explain her exceptional time of 5:54 in the 1989 Comrades marathon, and giving support to our belief that women have superior resistance to fatigue.

CONTROL OF BODY TEMPERATURE

Most of the factors which limit performance are readily accepted by most runners, who are generally content to run within them. However, one of the most important factors limiting endurance performance – that of the sustained elevation of muscle temperature during prolonged exercise – is often ignored, and its importance is underestimated.

During exercise, the conversion of chemical energy stored in the muscles into mechanical energy is extremely ineffi-cient, so that as much as 70% of the total chemical energy used during muscular contraction is released as heat, rather than as athletic endeavour.

Body mechanisms for heat loss

Because of the need for humans to keep body temperatures within a narrow range (35 to 42°C) to prevent either disastrous overheating (heatstroke), or excessive cooling (hypothermia due to exposure), the body is able to call upon a number of very effective mechanisms for regulating temperature. During exercise, these mechanisms aid heat loss. In addition, there are several practical ways in which runners can aid the heat-loss process. The two basic mechanisms used by the body to rid itself of unwanted heat are:

- direct heat loss to the cooler atmosphere (convection); and
- cooling due to evaporation of the sweat.

(A full description of the physiology of these mechanisms can be found in *Lore of Running*.)

Consideration of body heat loss is particularly important if you are able to run at close to world record pace for distances up to the half marathon. It appears that athletes running at this pace develop a marked limitation to skin blood flow, and therefore a limited ability to lose heat. Their ability to maintain heat equilibrium then depends entirely on the prevailing environmental conditions, and if these are unfavourable, the athletes will continually accumulate heat until their body temperatures reach the critical level at which heatstroke occurs. As a result of this, heatstroke occurs most commonly in fast short distance races (10-21 km) that are run in severe environmental conditions (i.e. air temperature greater than 28°C with high humidity).

Aids to heat loss

Environmental factors – atmospheric temperature, humidity and wind speed – are the primary determinants of the efficiency of body heat loss. Ways in which runners can aid the process include the appropriate choice of clothing, heat acclimatization, and sponging and drinking adequately during racing.

Clothing

Aesthetic reasons apart, the rationale for wearing clothing is to trap a thin layer of air next to the body. As air is a poor conductor of heat, this thin layer rapidly heats to body temperature, and acts as an insulator preventing heat loss. Clearly, when exercising in the heat, any clothing that is worn must be designed to have the opposite effect, in order to promote heat loss. This is best achieved by light porous clothing, such as 'fish net' vests. In contrast, T-shirts or heavy rugby jerseys act as very good insulators, which prevent adequate heat loss and thus impair performance. Water, unlike air, is a very good conductor of heat. Wetting the clothing, therefore, also aids heat loss.

There is seldom, if ever, the need for runners who live in moderate climates to train for any period in a tracksuit, although the mistaken belief that such a strategy might aid long-term weight loss prevails. By doing so, runners merely increase their own discomfort, produce more sweat, and promote conditions favourable for heatstroke. As soon as the exercise stops, the extra sweat (weight) loss will be rapidly replaced by fluid drunk by the runner.

Heat acclimatization

Only by exercising in the heat can a runner become heat-acclimatized. This is achieved relatively quickly, and is thought to be almost fully developed after seven to ten days. However, long-term adaptions (over decades or generations) may still occur, and might explain why those who live in hot, humid environments are probably at a competitive advantage during long-distance races run in hot conditions. Heat acclimatization is discussed further in Chapter 2.

Sponging

As skin temperature rises, it causes blood to pool in the veins of the arms and legs. This is because an elevated skin temperature 'paralyzes' the veins, which dilate and soon fill with a large volume of blood. This blood is effectively lost from the circulation and can only be returned if the skin temperature is reduced. This is achieved by sponging the skin and so lowering the skin temperature.

Drinking

Although it has recently been shown that dehydration is not the critical factor predisposing athletes to heatstroke during exercise, skin blood flow is reduced and body heat storage is increased by dehydration. Performance in the heat, but not the cold, is also impaired at fairly low levels of dehydration (less than 2% body weight loss). Conversely, drinking a

Refreshment stations are vital in marathons to enable runners to get sufficient fluid replenishment. Having your own personal service from a coach is even better, as Free State athlete Antoni Nyabanyaba discovers

glucose-electrolyte solution (preferably), or water during exercise enhances performance in the heat; less so during cold weather.

It is thus important that you drink sufficient fluid during intense exercise in the heat to avoid the effects of dehydration. 'Sufficient' is estimated at about 500-800 ml per hour, although sweat rate, and hence desirable replacement, will vary according to your body weight, running speed and also individual variability – athletes can be 'light' and 'heavy' sweaters. This is discussed further in Chapter 9.

Note that although it is possible to drink very large fluid volumes (greater than 1 l/hr) either at rest or during exercise, a large portion of that fluid is wasted, as it is not absorbed but is probably stored in the intestines. The maximum rate at which fluid can be absorbed seems to be about 800 ml/hour at rest and may be less during exercise. Unabsorbed fluid remains in the gut, and gives the athlete a bloated feeling.

Keeping warm

The problem of keeping warm while running is not often an issue for South African runners. However, it is important to take precautions if running in cold, wet and windy conditions. If the atmospheric temperature is colder than 6°C, and especially if there is a cold wind blowing, runners should wear layers of clothing, including a rainproof (but preferably breathable) outer jacket. Remember that wet clothing increases heat loss. Beginner runners who are starting out by alternating walking and running should also take care to keep warm when exercising in winter. A useful rule of the thumb is to wear what you will feel most comfortable in midway through your walk or run. Keep an extra tracksuit top or (if you have been running in the rain) a dry change of clothes handy if you are not able to go straight home to change after exercising.

Controlling body temperature: conclusions

The important practical advice for runners, then, is to keep their bodies at the optimum running temperature by following the above suggestions for keeping cool in the heat or relatively warm in cold weather.

Although the measures described above may be effective in aiding top performances, the most effective way to beat the heat in particular is to limit racing (at maximum effort) to when atmospheric conditions are favourable. The optimal racing temperature for the marathon is between 9-12°C; conditions which seldom apply in South Africa.

STYLE

We have all witnessed elite athletes whose running styles belie their running speed. Their limbs appear to flail in every direction, and their stumbling gait has the onlooker wondering how they are able to progress from point A to B, much less do so at a pace of 3 minutes per kilometre. Style can be highly deceptive, however; Matthews Motshwarateu, aptly nicknamed 'Loop-en-val' ('run-and-fall') because of his peculiar running style, was the first in the world to run 10 km on the road in under 28 minutes. His running style is clearly not as inefficient as it appears!

Theo Rafiri, who all but won the 1993 Comrades Marathon, eventually finishing second to German

Matthews 'Loop-en-val' Motshwarateu: his style belies his speed

marathoner Charly Doll, is another such case. His awkward sideways-leaning gait scarcely suggests that he could even complete 90 km on the road, let alone challenge for victory.

When former Australian marathon star Derek Clayton started training for marathon distances, his style changed naturally. He claimed that running 20 miles a day cut down on his stride length and eliminated his tendency to lift his knees. In the process, he developed what he called the 'Clayton Shuffle'. Two South African athletes who have excelled over marathon and ultramarathon distances, Sonja Laxton and Eric Bateman, have developed a similar shuffling gait. Alberto Salazar, winner of the 1994 Comrades Marathon, is another example of a runner with a superbly efficient shuffling gait.

A characteristic of these and other efficient runners is that they tend to 'glide' (or 'slide') along with very little discernible vertical movement. In this style, the airborne foot moves as close as possible to the ground – the opposite of an effective sprinting action. It is generally believed that this running style is more efficient and also leads to less muscle damage, especially during extremely prolonged exercise, such as running the Comrades Marathon.

AGE

Although many runners adopt a Canute-like attitude in attempting to hold back the tide of advancing years, it is a fact of life that runners, not unlike other mortals, age. Equally certain is that performance deteriorates with increasing age once a peak-performing age range has been reached.

What is less certain is the age at which peak performance is reached, and the extent to which performance declines thereafter. It has been established that in general, runners reach a peak between 20 and 30 years of age, and that there is a further noticeable decline in performance (especially in longer-distance races) after the age of 40 by those who have been running for many years.

Here, however, we must make the distinction between chronological age and years of running. A 40-year-old runner who has trained at high intensity for 20 or more years will experience greater difficulty maintaining his or her racing performance, than a 40-year-old with equal genetic ability who has only just started running competitively.

This is made abundantly clear when considering marathons and ultramarathons such as the Comrades. Those runners who dominated the race in their twenties and thirties, seldom maintain their supremacy in their forties. The best 40-year-olds were not generally dominant or active as competitive runners in their twenties and thirties, and do not maintain their age-group supremacy after the age of 60.

Although VO_2 max is not the sole determinant of running performance, it is interesting to note that the rate at which performance decreases over the age of 40 matches the rate at which the VO_2 max index declines.

Does regular exercise delay or slow down the inevitable ageing process if compared with a completely sedentary lifestyle? Studies show that healthy, but inactive subjects experience a gradual decline in VO_2 max of about 9% per decade after the age of 25. Encouragingly, there is evidence to suggest that regular exercise maintained for life may reduce the age-related rate of fall in VO_2 max to about 5% per decade in life-long athletes. We must bear in mind that these studies involve people participating in moderate amounts of exercise throughout their lives. The effect on the ageing process of more vigorous activities (such as marathon running) when maintained for life, is not yet known.

Studies also indicate that the greater the distance one races, the higher the peak performance age. However, this factor could be outweighed by the apparently greater decrease in speed in endurance running than in sprinting. Most older runners will have discovered this for themselves. They are able to run races of up to 10 km in times that are not too dissimilar from times they achieved when younger; but their times in marathons and longer-distance races fall off much more precipitously. We believe that this could be due to an age and running-related reduction in the ability of the body to absorb the shock of weight-bearing activities. As a result, very long distances can only be run at much slower speeds that do not generate the same levels of shock that the runner could comfortably sustain for many hours when younger.

We further believe that age-related speed loss in longer distance races is as much or more a function of 'running age' than absolute age. The number of years an athlete has been involved in competitive running is likely to be the key factor. Thus, a 50-year-old athlete who has recently taken up the sport is likely to find that his or her marathon time compares favourably with what it should be on the basis of his or her 800 m time. Another 50-year-old, who has been competing for 30 years, is likely to find that his or her marathon time is relatively worse than predicted from his or her 800 m times, compared to what they were 20 years ago.

There is uncertainty as to how ability over 10 km compares with ability over the marathon distance with increasing age. Statistics which express the South African veterans' records as a percentage of the seniors' records, suggest that the decline in performance with age (at least until the early forties) is similar for 10 km, 15 km, 21 km and 42 km. The respective percentages are 94%; 94%; 94%; and 93% respectively.

Of what practical use is this knowledge? In order to make a realistic judgement of our performance, it may be of interest to evaluate our performance in the light of expected physiological decline with increasing age. Figure 1.1 provides 'reference values' per age group for the standard marathon and the Comrades Marathon, based on world marathon and Comrades age group records.

These values, which are expressed as a fraction of performances for 25-30 year old athletes, can be used as an age handicapping system in marathon and ultra-marathon races. For example, if the winner in a particular standard marathon race is 25-30 years old and runs a time of 02:20:00, this would be regarded as the reference standard. To find

Elite athletes Danie Malan (left) and Geoff Tribe, now in their 40s, continue to enjoy running successes as veterans; Malan in cross-country and triathlon events, and Tribe in cross-country and road running

out how fast a 100-year-old runner competing in the same race would have to run in order to 'beat' the winner, the winning time should be divided by the reference value of the 100-year-old runner, i.e. 0,25. Thus, if our centenarian completed the race in a time faster than 09:20:00, his or her performance would be statistically better than that of the winner, and should be awarded first prize.

Obviously, similar reference values could be calculated if records were available for shorter distance events. An advantage of this type of handicapping system is that it operates independently of the difficulty of the course or the prevailing environmental conditions, as these will be the same for all the competitors. The first competitor to finish the race will be either helped or hindered by the environmental conditions or the nature of the course, and the index will automatically be corrected accordingly. (The only proviso would be that conditions do not undergo significant improvement or deterioration after the fastest runner completes the course.)

Even if this system is not in operation during a race, you could use it as a personal reference to check your performance on the basis of your age.

Figure 1.1
Age records for the male world standard marathon (Line B) and the Comrades (Line C) records. Line A = optimum prediction of performances, i.e., what results would be if more older runners participated and there were no sudden ageing effect at 65

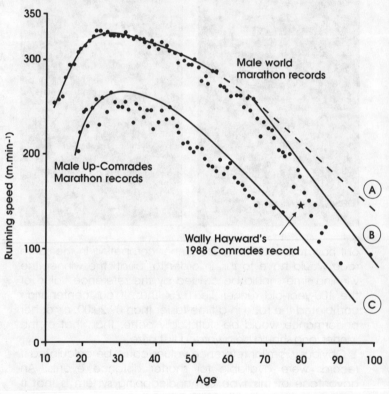

GENDER

The battle of the sexes has been waged in many areas of life, not least in the sporting arena! Although countless male runners have been soundly beaten many times by the top echelon of women athletes, it would appear that, in general, women will never run as fast as men.

Frith van der Merwe is an example of a female runner who has astounded many leading male athletes with her exceptional ultramarathon performances in recent years. She has beaten men who considered themselves potential champions. Her fifteenth place in the 1989 Comrades

Marathon, where she beat close to 12 000 runners, is a vivid example. World-class athlete Elana Meyer has taken overall line honours in mixed-gender events more than once, on one occasion walking away from a 15 km race with a lesser prize for 'first woman' than the one given to the 'first man', whom she had beaten fair and square! Nevertheless, Frith and Elana would be the first to admit that they could never beat top male athletes in peak condition, at least in races of up to 90-160 km. This prompts the question, why not?

Body fat

Although gender has no effect on running efficiency, females generally have lower VO_2 max values than males. This is because of their higher body fat content, their smaller muscle mass and, probably most significant, their less powerful muscles. Women have almost twice as much body fat as equally active men, the average percentage of body fat for women being 24% as opposed to an average 14% for men. Elite athletes have been measured at 8-10% for women and 3-5% for men. If one assumes that the muscle tissues of men and women have the same ability to consume oxygen, a woman is clearly disadvantaged when competing against a man of equal weight. As she has a higher percentage of body fat, she will have a lower muscle mass and hence a lower VO_2 max.

This difference in body fat and muscle mass, however, accounts for only 30% of the disparity in running performance between the sexes; the remainder is due to the superior muscle power of male athletes. The female muscle appears less able to produce speed or force during contraction than its male counterpart.

Resistance to fatigue

In spite of these facts, there are indications that women's muscles may be more resistant to fatigue than those of men, so that women may in fact have greater endurance than men. This idea first became popular in the 1970s, when it was suggested that the phenomenon of 'hitting the wall', in which runners experience the relatively sudden onset of fatigue about three-quarters of the way through a standard marathon (caused by many factors, including the depletion of muscle glycogen and the reduced shock-absorbing capacity of the muscles), seemed to be relatively unknown among women runners. A group of elite women marathoners, when interviewed, emphasized that this was an affliction which only affected the 'weaker sex'.

The suggestion that women are better able to metabolize their more abundant fat stores towards the end of a marathon now enjoys some scientific support; studies have shown that women burn more fat and less carbohydrate (specifically, less muscle glycogen) during exercise than equally fit men. As a result, women's muscle glycogen reserves will last longer than those of men when both run at the same intensity during prolonged exercise. The extent to which this could contribute to the better performance of women over longer-distance races is not yet known. A possible reason for the apparent strength of women athletes over longer distances may also be linked to mental toughness, or other as yet unknown factors. (It seems to be generally agreed that women have higher thresholds for enduring pain than men, and adapt more readily to physical stress.)

To investigate this question, Jenefer Bam, who has represented South Africa in international road-running competitions, compared the performances of men and women, at a range of racing distances, who completed the 1993 Two Oceans Marathon in comparable times. Her analysis showed that the men were significantly faster at all distances below 42 km, whereas the women performed better at distances greater than 56 km. In other words, the rate of decline in peak racing speed over increasing distance was greater in the male runners than in the female runners. Whereas the men were faster (more powerful) in the shorter distance races, the less-powerful women were more resistant to fatigue over increasing distance.

Will women surpass men?

These findings naturally raise the perennial question in the gender debate: will women one day surpass men in any running event? A superficial glance at the rapid improvement in women's long-distance records over the years compared with those of men seems to suggest that this may well be possible. However, the steeper performance curves in certain women's events are misleading. The rapid improvement in women's marathon times in the 1970s and 1980s represents a sociological, not a physiological phenomenon.

Jenefer Bam, sports science researcher, physiotherapist and top athlete, believes that women will prove themselves superior to men in exceptionally long-distance ultra-marathons

During the 1970s and 1980s, the number of women marathoners increased, better female athletes were attracted to the marathon, the event became more competitive, and the marathon record improved phenomenally. This rate of improvement clearly could not last, and was likely to slow down as the record became more representative of women's physiological limits. This has indeed happened, and no further improvement in the women's marathon record has occurred over the past decade. One can now safely predict that until women can run short distances as fast as men can, the curve showing future improvements in marathon times by women will remain lower than that representing men's achievements.

At present, it would appear that women are at least 6% slower than men over the popular race distances (up to 42 km) at which very large numbers of men and women compete internationally. A comparison between men's and women's 1991 world records indicates a difference of

The Kenyan athlete William Sigei after retaining his world cross-country title at Budapest in March 1994. Four months later, he went on to set a world 10 000 m track record which was bettered by Ethiopian Hailie Gebrselassie a year later

between 9% and 12% for most Olympic distances, the striking exception being provided by American sprinter, Florence Griffiths-Joyner. Griffiths-Joyner's record of 10,49 seconds in the 100 m event is just 6,6% off Donovan Bailey's record of 9,85 seconds, and her time of 21,34 seconds over 200 m is 8,2% off Pietro Mennea's best time of 19,72 seconds. Differences in endurance events from 800 m to the marathon vary from 8,3% in the 3 000 m to 12,7% in the 5 000 m. The difference in the standard marathon is 11,2%. The controversial performances of Chinese women athletes in 1993 have had a significant effect on closing the gap on male records in endurance events. Wang Junxia's 3 000 m mark of 8:06:11 is 10,3% off Daniel Komen's 7:20:67 world best, while her 10 000 m record of 29:31:78 is within 9,5% of Hailie Gebrselassie's 26:43:53, set in 1995.

Nevertheless, our prediction based on the findings of Jenefer Bam's study, amongst others, is that these differences will diminish as the race distance extends beyond 42 km. It is interesting to note that Frith van der Merwe's Comrades Marathon record for the 'down' run of 5:54:43 is within 9,2% of Bruce Fordyce's 5:24:07 down record. Ultimately, there must be a racing distance at which the superior fatigue resistance of women will give them the edge over men who are faster at shorter distances. Unfortunately, the race distances at which this will happen are probably well over 400 km – races that are not frequently contested. Until they are, men will no doubt persist with the erroneous belief that they are better runners than women under all conditions!

In summary, we should be aware of how the physiological differences between men and women influence performance. As a general rule of thumb, women can expect to run to within 8% to 15% of times achieved by male athletes of similar stature in races of up to 42 km; however, these differences will become increasingly smaller as the racing distance increases.

HEREDITARY TRAITS

We have already seen that VO_2 max values for elite athletes can be as high as 85 ml/kg/min, while average athletes typically have values ranging from 45 to 55 ml/kg/min. We also know that VO_2 max can be improved by an average of only 5-15%, even with intensive training, so it is clear that even with a strenuous training programme of six hours a day, the average healthy individual will never achieve a VO_2 max value anywhere near those of elite athletes. While the reliability of VO_2 max as a performance indicator has been called into question (see p. 12), elite athletes nevertheless tend to have relatively high VO_2 max starting levels, which then increase by more than the average 5-15% with training. In some elite runners, the increase may be as great as 50-60%. It would thus seem that hereditary factors do largely determine who will become champions.

The extent to which any individual can adapt to an endurance training programme (more about this in Chapter 3), and the rapidity with which this adaptation takes place, is genetically determined. It has been found that there are high and low responders to training, the low responders showing little, if any, improvement with training regardless of how hard they try.

Thus, elite athletes are successful because, first and foremost, their genetic make-up is such that they have the right 'machinery' to begin with; secondly, they will 'adapt' to the greatest possible extent through training. These are not the only factors determining success (the ability to harness mental strength and to understand and implement the principles of training are also important); without them, however, an athlete will be unable to reach the elite level.

NUTRITION: control of the fuel source

Studies have shown that those who exercise vigorously have a natural tendency to eat foods which provide their bodies with adequate, if not optimal, nutritional resources. The legendary ultramarathon runner Arthur Newton supports this with his belief that 'the only definite dietary rule ... would be "eat what you like". Nature generally knows what is needed, and what is needed is right. Satisfy your digestion with anything you seem to fancy and you need have no qualms.'

Regardless of how true this may be, nutrition appears to be one of the most neglected areas in the quest to find our optimal potential as runners. We tend to spend considerable time and energy seeking and following the ideal training programme but are inclined to neglect aspects such as nutrition, which may be perceived as peripheral to the primary task of 'training'.

It is a law of nature that for work to be done, energy must be expended. The internal combustion engine is dependent on fuel to transfer one form of energy into a more usable kind – in the case of the motor car, chemical energy released from the combustion of petrol is converted into potential and kinetic energy. Our bodies operate on the identical principle. To carry out work, energy derived from food must be converted into the body's energy 'currency' and transported to the site at which the chemical energy is converted into mechanical energy in the muscles.

Carbohydrate-loading prior to a race is one aspect of diet which is followed religiously by many runners, but it is important to have a more holistic understanding of our nutritional requirements. An awareness of the different food groups, and an understanding of their role in our habitual training diet will enable us to eat those foods which are conducive to optimal running performance. The body requires, in appropriate quantities, energy-supplying nutrients (carbohydrates, fats and proteins), as well as those nutrients needed to utilize the energy (vitamins, minerals, trace elements and water). Failure to achieve an adequate nutrient balance in our diets will adversely affect performance. How to adapt our diet for optimal running performance is covered in Chapter 8.

DRUGS: the good, the bad and the ugly

Any doubts about the effectiveness of drugs in aiding running performance has been dispelled by a number of recent events. The second banning of Ben Johnson occurred after he had resumed taking steroids following his initial two-year ban after the 1988 Olympic Games. Johnson had discovered that without steroids, he simply was not able to perform at a sufficiently competitive level.

There have also been widespread allegations that the East Germans had discovered that low doses of steroids could aid the training of distance runners, by allowing them to do more training at a higher intensity, and to recover more quickly.

More recently, there have been suggestions that the remarkable successes of the up-and-coming Chinese women runners stem more from their sophisticated knowledge of the use of performance-enhancing drugs, than from their rigorous training or natural ability. A more reasonable opinion would be that even if drugs were involved, they could not supply the whole explanation. For one, even though drug use was almost certainly widespread among the East German women runners (this abuse has been confirmed by the International Amateur Athletics Federation), their records were surpassed by the Chinese athletes. Thus, something more than drugs must be involved in the achievements of the latter. Genetic ability, living and training at altitude, an exceptionally heavy training programme, and perhaps a different mental approach to sport and competition, are all possible factors that must be considered when the success of the Chinese women runners is debated.

It cannot be stressed strongly enough that drugs taken purely to enhance performance are anathema in running. Their use debases the sport, which becomes a competition not between athletes, but between the pharmaceutical companies that manufacture performance-enhancing drugs, as well as agents able to mask the presence of drugs in athletes. Those who choose to use drugs to enhance their performance must be exposed as cheats and expelled from the sport. They have no place in competitive running if the honesty and credibility of the sport is to be preserved.

Stimulants

However, drug-testing in sport becomes a problem for honest athletes when it identifies their use of legitimate medications that also happen to be banned. The most famous South African example is the case of Charl Mattheus, who was the first to finish the 1992 Comrades Marathon. His post-race urine sample contained traces of the banned stimulant phenylpropanalomine.

Before testing, Mattheus reported that in the days leading up to the race he had used the over-the-counter 'flu

Charl Mattheus, whose innocent use of 'flu medication led to an unlucky dope charge, together with Frith van der Merwe after they had won the Foot of Africa marathon

preparation Degoran for the treatment of a minor inter-current illness. He claimed to have taken the last dose at least 12 hours before the race; i.e. more than 18 hours before his urine sample was collected.

Besides the stimulant phenylpropanalomine, Degoran contains the antihistamine chlorpheniramine which has a sedative (sleep-inducing) effect; in fact, the accompanying leaflet warns of possible drowsiness as a result of use. This particular preparation would thus seem to be an improbable choice for a prospective cheat wishing to enhance his performance during the Comrades Marathon.

Stimulated by the obvious uncertainties generated by this case, Dr Hunter Gillies, a student in our research laboratory at UCT, recently completed a study of the effects of exercise on urinary excretion of a single dose of the stimulant, pseudo-ephedrine. This agent, similar to phenylpropanalomine, accounts for a large number of the 'positive' dope tests in this country, as it is present in many over-the-counter 'flu preparations. Dr Gillies also wished to determine whether pseudoephedrine aids performance during high intensity exercise of relatively short duration (approximately an hour).

Not unexpectedly, he found that psedoephedrine did not influence performance during a 40-kilometre cycling time trial in the laboratory. No study has yet shown that stimulants, with the exception of the amphetamines (banned and illegal) and caffeine (not banned), have a perfor-mance-enhancing effect. Stimulants are banned because they have certain effects in common with amphetamines, and could possibly aid performance. In a sense, most stimulants are banned because of an absence of evidence proving that they do not work, rather than firm evidence proving their efficacy.

Second, Dr Gillies showed that post-exercise urinary pseudoephedrine concentrations of some individuals reached levels previously reported only in those who had died of pseudoephedrine poisoning. Blood levels, however, were not abnormally high. Hence exercise increases in some unknown way the rate at which drugs taken before exercise are excreted in the urine.

This raises the question of whether exercise – especially if it is exceptionally prolonged, as in the Comrades – might falsely identify the presence of drugs last taken some days before competing. It is possible that detectable concentra-tions of drugs might reappear in the urine after very prolonged exercise, even though the athlete had stopped taking the agent many days before competition.

Antidepressants (Prozac)

Another intriguing drug-related issue was raised by Alberto Salazar's stunning victory in the 1994 Comrades Marathon. Salazar's running career had been on hold for more than ten years since he had been the world's dominant marathon runner (including the world record holder), and a formidable 10 000 m runner with a best time of 27:29 in the early 1980s.

Following his third victory in the New York Marathon in 1982, Salazar had suffered from an increased susceptibility to intercurrent infections, an inability to run at the same competitive level as before, and eventually increasing difficulty with completing even a daily training run of 5-10 km.

In 1992, Salazar's physician prescribed the antidepressant medication Prozac, which had helped other runners with symptoms similar to those experienced by Salazar. The results were spectacular. Within a short time, Salazar was once again able to train as he had done previously – up to 200 or more km per week, with a good scattering of speedwork. (Although he believes he has as much endurance as in the past, Salazar feels that his speed is not what it once was. This is borne out by his present best 10 km time, which is still about two minutes slower than his best time set 12 years ago.)

Prozac is not a banned substance; should it now be added to the banned list? The answer is almost certainly no. Unlike anabolic steroids, it is a legitimate medication used to treat real medical problems. Furthermore, it is unlikely to enhance performance to a level beyond that which is limited by the runner's natural ability. Salazar is not running better than he did in the 1980s; he is running only as well as one would predict a former marathon world-record holder to be running at the age of 35. Until there is evidence that this agent would have improved the performances of Salazar and others when they were young and at the peak of their physical abilities, there is no reason to prevent athletes with legitimate medical reasons from using these agents under appropriate medical supervision. In fact, all the current evidence suggests that antidepressant agents impair the exercise performance of healthy athletes. Why Salazar experienced the opposite effect remains an intriguing mystery.

Alberto Salazar, former world record holder for the marathon, has also been unfairly accused of drug abuse. Here he makes his sensational debut win at the 1994 Comrades

Terfitus Pickard, South African Sports Illustrated

Advice for runners and administrators

The advice to runners is absolutely clear. To be completely certain of a negative drug test, no medications containing banned substances must be taken during the four days leading up to any competition; perhaps for an even longer period before prolonged events such as the Comrades Marathon.

Administrators, meanwhile, should exercise considerable caution until more is known about the effects of very pro-longed exercise on the excretion patterns of drugs, and act with circumspection when confronted with 'positive' doping cases in circumstances similar to those surrounding the Mattheus case. Some would argue that many of these points apply equally to the actions taken against Argentinean soccer player Diego Maradonna, whose urine was found to contain a number of stimulants, including pseudoephedrine, following a match in the 1994 soccer World Cup.

Finally, a summary of banned substances is listed in Appendix 1 (see pp. 206-10).

2 WHAT DETERMINES PERFORMANCE?

External factors

Any runner will agree that running into the wind in soft sand up a steep hill 2 000 m above sea level, wearing heavy boots, at the hottest time of the day, is hard work! It would certainly be much easier to coast down a gentle incline in racing flats at the coast. Altitude, topography, terrain, wind resistance, weather, time of day, leg-weight, and clothing all play a decisive role in determining running performance. Having looked at the role of physiological factors that affect your body in Chapter 1, we turn now to examine the influence of external factors on running performance.

ALTITUDE

Any runner who lives close to sea-level, and has attempted to race at altitude, will be aware of the difficulties of strenuous exercise when there is less oxygen in the air than he or she is accustomed to. Athletes experience these effects in various ways. Some are unaware of any undue physiological hardships, but find that they simply cannot run as quickly over distances in excess of a kilometre as they are used to doing. Others feel a rasping of air in their chest and dizziness, and find that continuing to run brings severe discomfort.

Because of reduced wind resistance, sprinters run faster at medium altitude, up to 3 000 m. There is no doubt, however, that performances in races lasting more than two minutes are impaired at altitudes in excess of 1 000 m. It is equally certain that athletes who have not acclimatized to the effects of altitude are at a disadvantage when competing against those who have, and even more so when competing against athletes who were born at and who have always lived at altitude, so-called 'altitude natives'. It also appears that in certain athletes, who allow the altitude 'bogey' to loom larger than reality, these adverse physiological effects are compounded by a concurrent psychological reaction, which reduces performance still further.

The ultramarathon legend, Arthur Newton, may have fallen prey to this malady, in spite of his mental toughness: 'At 6000 ft, Johannesburg, I was all but incapable as a runner: my marathon time there was in the region of three and a half hours and the effort left me considerably distressed – for hours afterwards I was seized with fits of gulping like a fish out of water.'

While we are not certain exactly why performance is impaired at altitude in races lasting longer than two minutes, it is probable that the lack of oxygen either acts directly to impair muscle contractility or power (the muscles thus become less powerful), or causes the athlete's blood lactate levels to rise more rapidly and to reach peak levels which indirectly limit performance at lower running speeds than at sea level. This could explain the common shortness-of-breath syndrome at altitude: runners who try to run at the same speeds as at sea level often become excessively short of breath because their blood lactate levels, which indirectly influence breathing, are higher than usual. Thus their perception of effort is increased at altitude.

In order to make a realistic assessment of your probable competitive performance level at altitude, you should increase your expected (coastal) time by a factor. The extent to which performance is reduced (by whatever means) in races of different durations at different altitudes is shown in Table 2.1.

Sea-level athletes are always at a disadvantage when competing at altitude against altitude residents in events lasting longer than two minutes. This is because sea-level athletes suffer a dramatic fall in work performance and in VO_2 max as soon as they arrive at altitude and this reduction corrects only slowly.

The practical implications are that sea-level athletes who must compete at altitude should compete either the moment they arrive at altitude, or only after they have been living at that altitude for three or more weeks; three months is preferable. For this reason sporting teams from the coast have given up the practice, when possible, of arriving the night before a competition. The worst time to compete at altitude is within three to six days after first arriving at that altitude.

Table 2.1
Performances equivalent to sea-level records for men and women at different altitudes

Location	Sea-level	Munich	Calgary/ Bloem- fontein	Alber- querque	Colorado Springs/ Johannes- burg	Mexico City	La Paz	
Altitude (m)	0	500	1 000	1 500	1 800	2 240	3 658	4 000
Men								
60 m	6,41	6,39	6,37	6,35	6,34	6,32	6,28	6,27
100 m	9,92	9,88	9,83	9,79	9,77	9,74	9,66	9,64
200 m	19,75	19,64	19,52	19,43	19,37	19,30	19,12	19,10
400 m	43,29	43,14	42,97	42,84	42,76	42,70	42,96	43,16
800 m	1:41,73	1:42,11	1:42,40	1:42,73	1:43,07	1:43,71	1:48,67	1:50,78
1 500 m	3:29,46	3:31,24	3:32,76	3:34,33	3:35,71	3:38,10	3:54,10	4:00,64
1 609 m	3:46,32	3:50,05	3:50,05	3:51,82	3:53,37	3:56,04	$:13,82	4:21,06
5 000 m	12:58,39	13:09,07	13:18,61	13:28,14	13:36,16	13:49,58	15:14,93	15:49,28
10 000 m	27:08,23	27:32,52	27:54,36	28:15,97	28:34,00	29:03,89	32:10,83	33:25,38
Marathon	2:06:50,00	2:08:57,58	2:10:52,93	2:12:46,21	2:14:19,67	2:16:53,15	2:32:37,87	2:38:52,13
Women								
60 m	7,00	6,97	6,94	6,92	6,90	6,88	6,82	6,81
100 m	10,49	10,44	10,38	10,33	10,30	10,27	10,16	10,14
200 m	21,34	21,20	21,06	20,95	20,87	20,78	20,56	20,53
400 m	47,60	47,43	47,24	47,08	47,00	46,94	47,29	47,53
800 m	1:53,28	1:53,75	1:54,11	1:54,53	1:54,94	1:55,72	2:01,64	2:04,17
1 500 m	3:52,47	3:54,50	3:56,26	3:58,06	3:59,64	4:02,37	4:20,67	4:28,15
1 609 m	4:15,80	4:18,17	4:20,22	4:22,33	4:24,16	4:27,33	4:48,43	4:57,05
5 000 m	14:37,33	14:49,65	15:00,67	15:11,67	15:20,92	15:36,40	17:14,89	17:54,58
10 000 m	30:13,74	30:40,99	31:05,49	31:29,74	31:49,95	32:23,46	35:53,04	37:16,63
Marathon	2:21:06,00	2:23:28,42	2:25:37,22	2:27:43,72	2:29:28,12	2:32:19,58	2:49:55,60	2:56:54,31

Ideally, the athlete who lives at sea-level and who is obliged to compete at altitude, should undergo at least some short-term altitude acclimatization. However, while top athletes world-wide continue to utilize altitude training in the hope that it will enhance their performances in races at sea-level, this wisdom is questionable.

The problem with training at altitude is that because of the reduced oxygen content in the air, athletes are never able to train quite as fast or intensively as they would at sea-level. Thus, when training at altitude, their racing fitness for sea-level competition falls slightly, despite their enhanced ability to perform at altitude. If athletes could arrange to live at altitude and train at the coast, maximum benefit would be realized. Some reports are available on research into devices, fitted to athletes while they sleep, which simulate conditions at altitude by reducing the levels of available oxygen. This apparently has the same effect on the user of living at altitude.

In order to be fair to all participants, all championship races in excess of two minutes duration should be held at the coast. The former South African Road Runners Association took this step five years ago, while the national cross-country body made the same decision in 1991. Track and Field have not yet followed suit, although South Africa's return to international athletics, where all major track meetings are held at sea level, could force their hand.

TOPOGRAPHY

'It doesn't matter how much time you lose on the uphills; you can always make it up on the downs,' is a statement frequently, but erroneously, bandied about by optimistic runners at the start of hilly races. It has been shown, in fact, that approximately twice as much energy is expended when running up steep gradients as is saved on equivalent downward slopes.

More precisely, uphill running increases oxygen cost by about 2,6 ml 02/kg/min for each 1% increase in gradient. This is roughly equivalent to a reduction in running speed of about 0,65 km/hr. In comparison, downhill running reduces the oxygen cost of running by about 1,5 ml 02/kg/min for each 1% gradient, equivalent to an increase in speed of about 0,35 km/hr.

What practical value does this information have? Firstly, it indicates that time lost going up a hill can never be fully regained by running an identical downhill gradient. Secondly, the data in Figure 2.1 can be used to estimate how much time you can expect to lose or gain on a particular section of a race if the gradient of that section is known. This will enable you to set a more realistic goal for the race and to pace yourself accordingly, thus avoiding a major 'blow' in the latter stages of the race.

Are the fastest courses the flattest? In theory, this should be the case, although there is some doubt as to whether this is actually so. Many elite athletes favour a gently undulating, rather than a 'pancake' course, particularly over distances

Vaal Triangle marathoner Elias Stemmer tackles unfavourable running conditions: a steep gradient over rough terrain on a very hot day. He overcame the treble handicap to win the first of his four foot of Africa marathon titles

greater than 21 km. The inclines bring additional muscle groups into play, while affording the overtaxed ones some rest. We know that running uphill is a specific discipline which stresses specific muscles more than downhill running, or even running on flat gradients. Whether resting these muscle groups for short intervals results in physiological benefit is uncertain. It may, however, bring about an overall performance benefit through psychological factors; i.e., the perception that the muscle is resting enables the athlete to run faster. A course of varying gradient is also easier to visualize (see Chapter 7). It would seem that a course with a few short, relatively steep uphills combined with long gradual down-sloping gradients may prove optimum for the standard marathon.

TERRAIN

The influence of the running surface on the oxygen cost of running was first studied in 1955 by scientists who reported that the oxygen cost of walking across a ploughed field was 35% greater than the cost of walking at the same speed on a smooth, firm surface. Subsequent studies have shown that running on sand has a similar effect. Famous Australian coach Percy Cerutty recognized this, and subjected his athletes to frequent training sessions on loose sand.

More recently, detailed attention has been given to the composition of track running surfaces. By optimizing the spring constant of a track, running performance and running economy will improve. The synthetic substance currently enjoying favour, and which was used to build the tracks for the 1992 Olympic Games, markets itself not only as the 'fastest' in the world, but also, due to its resilience, the least likely to cause injury.

The fact that varying terrain results in differences in running efficiency explains why the fastest track or road athletes are not necessarily the best at cross-country, particularly when the surface is rough or yielding. Endurance and agility are factors which, together with speed, make a top cross-country runner.

WIND RESISTANCE

In 1989 Mandla Mtombu, a talented Transvaal marathoner, won the Peninsula Marathon between Green Point and Simon's Town in 2:26:43 – one of the slowest ever winning times and a full 15 minutes outside the course record. The most important factor responsible for the slow times that year was the near gale force south-easterly wind into which the race was run.

It has been calculated that the cost of running into a head wind increases approximately as the square of the wind speed (Figure 2.1). The oxygen cost of running into a 62 km/hr headwind is increased by some 32 ml O_2/kg/min, which translates into a reduction in running speed of 8 km/hr. Thus, by running into a headwind which blew consistently at 36 km/hr directly against him, thereby reducing his running speed by 2,5 km/hr, Mtombu's effort was equivalent to world record pace!

The effect of a tailwind, meanwhile, has been shown to be about half that of a facing wind (although obviously in the opposite direction).

The wind-related speed reduction figures indicated by the graph are of limited practical value, however. To translate the speed reduction into total race time, you must assume that wind speed and direction will remain constant throughout the race, something which never happens in reality.

Figure 2.1
The additional oxygen costs of running up steep gradients or into facing winds

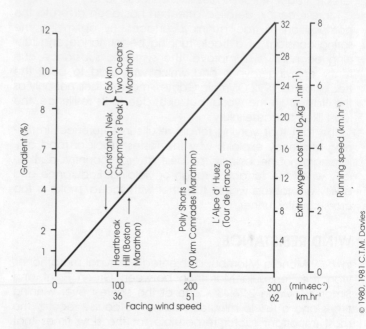

Mtombu would be the first to concede that his run could not be judged by world record standards!

Nevertheless, understanding wind resistance theory is of considerable practical value for track runners. At the speed at which middle-distance track events are run (6 m/s or about 67 seconds per 400 m), about 8% of the runner's energy is used in overcoming air resistance. By running directly behind a runner at a distance of about 1 m, athletes can save themselves 80% of that energy. In a middle-distance race, this would be equivalent to a saving of about four seconds per lap. Although it is unlikely that in practice the following athletes would ever be able to run consistently close enough to the lead runner to benefit to this extent, by running slightly to the side of the runner in front, the following runner would probably benefit by about one second a lap, or about 25 seconds over 10 000 m. Further research suggests that at world record pace for the mile, running 2 m behind the lead runner would effect an energy saving of about 1,66 seconds a lap.

John September (rear) enjoys a 'free ride' behind Thabang Baholo and Owen MacHelm in the Worcester half-marathon. Studies have shown that drafting like this can save important seconds

These findings clearly explain why track athletes find pacers such an essential ingredient in their attempts at world track records. They also explain why world records in the sprints are set at altitude. This is because during sprinting, the energy cost of overcoming air resistance rises to between 13-16% of the total cost of running. Thus, the sprinter benefits greatly by running at altitude, where air resistance is considerably reduced.

The most dramatic proof of this fact came during the 1968 Olympic Games at Mexico City (altitude 2 240 m), where world records were achieved in all sprint events shorter than 800 m. In the men's 800 m, the record was equalled. The World Track Championships are scheduled for Mexico City in 1997, and once again it is expected that the sprint records will be rewritten. In the short term, however, these records are likely to be beaten only on tracks that are at altitude equal to, or higher than Mexico City.

It is also interesting to note that according to various studies, an athlete's optimum strategy, when racing on a circular track, is to accelerate into the wind and to decelerate when the wind is from behind, the opposite to what might be expected.

Is wind resistance an important factor for road athletes? It has been shown that on a calm day, anyone running slower than 18 km/hr (about a 2:21 marathon pace) will not benefit by drafting in the wake of other runners. However, runners stand to gain considerably by drafting when running at faster speeds, or when running into winds that, when added to their running speeds, would make the effective wind speed greater than 18 km/hr.

The world marathon record is run at a pace of about 20 km/hr, and if your intention is to set a world marathon record, you would be well advised to draft for as much of the race as possible. Front-running in the marathon is almost as wasteful of energy as front-running on the track, whereas drafting in a tightly-knit bunch at world marathon pace would increase your speed by 0.82 km/hr – equivalent to a reduction in racing time of 4 minutes! It can only be assumed that as this fact becomes more widely recognised, we shall see pacers in marathon races as well as in track races.

Apart from drafting, there are other ways of reducing wind resistance. The importance of dressing in aerodynamic clothing has increasingly been recognized, particularly in sprint events. Experiments have shown that the following factors increase the aerodynamic drag experienced by the runner: shoes with exposed laces (0,5%); hair on limbs (0,6%); long socks (0,9%); short hair (4%); loosely-fitting clothing (4,2%) and long hair (6,3%). By reducing aerodynamic drag by as little as 2%, equivalent to a short hair cut, you would reduce your running time over 100 m by 0,01 seconds, and in a standard marathon by 5,7 seconds.

WEATHER CONDITIONS

The 1991 56 km Two Oceans Marathon took place on one of the hottest days in the history of the race. Temperatures reached 33°C. It is no coincidence that Miltas Tshabalala's winning time of 3:16:00 was the slowest in 11 years, and that most runners recorded poor times. This underlines the fact that runners cannot perform optimally in high temperatures.

Although we do not yet know the extent to which racing performance is affected at higher environmental temperatures, it would appear that a dry bulb temperature of between 9 and 13°C is optimum for the marathon. This is in line with the world male and female marathon records, both of which were set at dry bulb temperatures of between 10 and 12°C.

It has been calculated that at temperatures higher than 25°C, marathon finishing times will be 7 to 10% slower than races run at 10°C. The world's best marathon athletes met at the 1991 World Championships in Tokyo, but the winning time by local runner Hiromi Taniguchi of 2:14:57 was some 8 minutes off world record pace. This was because the marathon took place in unfavourably hot and humid conditions. American Steve Spence, who was not expected to finish among the leading athletes, took third position in 2:15:36 because he anticipated the heat and paced himself accordingly, moving through the field during the later stages of the race.

Similarly, prior to the Barcelona Olympic Games marathons, which were run in temperatures of between 28-32°C, we advised the coaches of the South African marathon teams that the winning times in both the male and female races would be about 7% slower than the world record (calculated as an 0.54% reduction in the time for each 1°C above 15°C). This predicted winning times of 2:15 in the men's event and 2:31 in the women's event, both of which proved remarkably accurate. The prediction for the women's event was 1:41 faster than the 2:32:41 run by Russian Valentina Yegorova, while the men's prediction was 1:37 too slow. Perhaps the fact that the women's event was won by a European, perhaps unadapted to hot-weather running, whereas the men's race was won in 2:13:23 by Korean athlete, Hwang Young-cho, who lives and trains in a hot environment, would explain the slight errors on either side.

By taking the starting line test (if you do not feel cold in your skimpy running gear, it is too warm to run for a fast time) and knowing the likely dry bulb temperature that will be reached during the race, you can estimate your finish time more realistically and pace yourself accordingly.

A significant problem for many runners is that most of our training is done in the cooler times of the day, either in the early mornings or late evenings. The result is that we are not adequately acclimatized for exercise in the heat, because we have not trained sufficiently in warm weather conditions.

Warren Petterson (left) models the ideal warm-weather running vest: fine-mesh netting material, cut short for maximum aeration, while Soulman Nakedi covers up with a long-sleeved thermal top in the 1994 Riebeeckberg marathon, run in winter

Thus, we will fail to realise our running potential when we have to run in the heat. If you are likely to race in hot weather, it is advisable to undergo a period of heat acclimatization. This can be achieved quite rapidly. Five to eight exercise sessions on consecutive days in the heat, each of up to two hours, produce optimum short-term acclimatization which lasts for some weeks. Living and training in a hot environment for months, or even years may be necessary to achieve complete heat acclimatization.

Other weather conditions which effect performance are humidity and wind. Humidity affects racing performance to the extent that it affects the body's heat controlling mechanism (discussed on p. 18), while the role of wind has been discussed above.

TIME OF DAY

Some research has been done on the effects on athletic performance of competing at various times of the day. It is known, however, that the body has a well-established 24-hour (circadian) rhythm. A study of the parameters which determine athletic performance suggests that you are likely to run your best between noon and 21h00. The ability to exercise declines to a minimum between 03h00 and 06h00.

Your performances can therefore be expected to be superior in the afternoon, and you are theoretically less likely to produce personal best times in early morning races, than in an afternoon event with identical conditions. This should be offset against the fact that for most of the year in South Africa, weather conditions are likely to be more favourable in the early morning.

If the race is to be run at a time of day at which you do not normally train, it would be helpful to do at least some training at that particular time of day.

LEG WEIGHT AND CLOTHING

Many of us have experienced performance benefits through substituting our weighty training shoes for lighter, less protective racing flats. We are prepared to risk injury in the quest for extra speed on race day. But does this easing of the burden on our feet make us more efficient runners?

Extra weight added to our legs or feet would appear to have a substantial effect on our running economy. Studies have shown that the addition of 0,5 kg to each thigh or to each foot increases the oxygen cost of running by 3,5% and 7,2% respectively. Other research has shown that the addition of 1 kg to our feet increases the oxygen cost of running by between 6% and 10%, or about 1% per 100 g increase in the weight of footwear.

Clearly, a 1% saving in energy expenditure during a standard 42 km marathon race is not inconsiderable. If this is translated directly into a 1% improvement in performance, it would mean a saving of 77 seconds at world record marathon pace. Nevertheless, the assumption that this energy saving will cause an equivalent improvement in running performance has yet to be proven. In-shoe orthotics used in the treatment of a number of running injuries will also increase shoe weight, and would therefore be expected to adversely influence running economy.

Clothing can also be expected to influence running efficiency, both in terms of wind resistance (see above) and weight. Calculations on the influence of additional clothing weight on racing performance vary, but this influence is slight in comparison with that of the weight of shoes. Indications are that world-class athletes can expect to improve their marathon time by between 5 and 15 seconds by switching from a cotton (weight 234 g) to a nylon vest (weight 150 g). The improvement would be almost double for a 4-hour marathoner.

3 WHAT DETERMINES PERFORMANCE?
Training

In Chapter 1, we looked at 'internal' or genetically-determined factors which limit our performance as runners. By and large, these factors are beyond our power to change. Apart from age (which is beyond our control and changing constantly: we are all getting older!) and nutrition, all of these factors have hereditary roots. If we are dissatisfied with our running speed as a consequence of our VO₂ max, our muscle contractility, or our gender, for the most part we can only blame our parents.

In Chapter 2, we discussed the role of external factors in determining our ability to run our best. We noted that factors such as altitude, weather conditions, terrain and topography can seriously limit our prospects of breaking world records. Although we can control these factors to the extent that we can choose not to run in disadvantageous conditions, we are bound by the laws of nature if we wish to compete in races which are held under sub-optimal circumstances, and our performance times will suffer accordingly. (Our performance relative to others, however, can improve if we learn to run within the limitations imposed by these external factors. The clever athlete who plans carefully is the one who benefits the most from unfavourable conditions.)

Unlike the first two chapters, where we looked at performance factors which mostly relate either to events which took place prior to our birth, or fall into the 'Acts of God' category, this chapter discusses one performance variable which is directly under our control: training. Whereas the apparent predestined nature of our competitive potential (outlined in Chapters 1 and 2) may lead to pessimism concerning our own potential improvement, Chapter 3 rekindles hope that through training we can indeed attain new heights in our running career.

There are many examples of runners who suddenly improve as a result of harnessing appropriate training techniques. What, for example, enabled Ron Boreham, little more than a 'useful' club athlete in Cape Town who regularly clocked an average of 2:35 for the standard marathon, to move up a gear and within two years run one of the fastest marathons ever recorded in South Africa (2:12)?

What further increases our competitive interest in running is the inability of science to accurately predict our athletic potential. We know now, for example, that maximum oxygen consumption (VO_2 max), once thought to be an accurate indicator of potential running ability is not the only or even the most important factor involved. Running efficiency, fatigue resistance (see Chapter 1), and, most important of all, correct training methods (aimed at both physical and mental strengthening) also determine performance. There is therefore every incentive to work hard on those factors which can make a difference.

TRAINING: control of body fitness

The 'how' of training is discussed in some detail in Chapters 4, 5 and 6. Here we are concerned with the 'why' of training, and its role in determining and improving running performance.

The importance of training for running your best goes without saying. Clearly, we will be able to run further and faster if we persuade our bodies to adapt to increased work loads through training. The initial effects of training are direct: the more we train, the further (and possibly faster) we will be able to run. Unfortunately, however, this process will not continue indefinitely.

Firstly, there is a limit to the amount of stress in the form of training load that our bodies can absorb before breakdown and injury results. Secondly, as mentioned in the previous chapter, there is a small percentage of 'low responders' who are genetically disadvantaged, and who adapt poorly to training. After the initial improvement brought about by the change from an inactive and possibly unhealthy lifestyle, the rewards for these people will be minimal, regardless of much they train. For most beginner runners, however, there are readily discernible and gratifying improvements, as well as ongoing benefits associated with increased fitness.

Physiological adaptations to training
Increased VO₂ max

The potential for increasing your VO_2 max through training is limited. At the most, the normal runner can expect to increase his or her VO_2 max by between 5 and 15%. This again demonstrates that VO_2 max is in fact a poor indicator of fitness, as one's ability to run both longer and faster will increase by more than 15% with training.

Of course, there are some lucky runners who will show more than a 5-15% increase in VO_2 max with training. For example, former mile world record holder, Jim Ryun, increased his VO_2 max from 65 ml O_2/kg/min in the partially trained state, to 82 ml O_2/kg/min in the trained state, a whopping 26% increase. This once again emphasizes that ability of the elite athlete to show a greater adaptation to training response. Most of the increase in VO_2 max is due to an increase in muscle contractility, which increases the capacity of the muscles to produce power (see Chapter 1, p. 11-12).

We would encourage you not to become pessimistic about your chances of improving your running ability simply on the basis of a relatively low VO_2 max.

Running economy

Running economy or efficiency, discussed in Chapter 1, is all-important. Can training really make us more efficient runners? It appears that both people beginning to exercise and those who are already trained to some degree do become more efficient through training, partly due to weight loss. A further part of this improved efficiency may relate to a change in running style, or adaptation to some of the limiting physical conditions discussed in Chapter 2. Probably more significant, however, are the various metabolic adaptations which come about with training and which probably explain the increased fatigue resistance characteristic of the highly-trained endurance athlete.

Three such metabolic adaptations are: (i) an increased capacity to store carbohydrate or muscle glycogen; (ii) an increased rate of fat oxidation as glycogen utilization decreases; and (iii) a shift in the lactate turnpoint to a higher running speed. As a result of these adaptations, fatigue resistance during prolonged exercise is increased. How can knowledge of these adaptations assist us in our quest to run our best?

Blanche Moila, one of South Africa's trail-blazing female athletes, exhibits the physical and mental power brought about by training

Storage capacity of muscle glycogen

Glycogen is the only form in which both the muscles and the liver store dietary carbohydrates. This energy-giving substance is stored in muscle tissue in the form of long-branching chains of glucose molecules and is used up progressively as one exercises. Training improves the ability of muscle tissue to store glycogen, thus providing the athlete with greater energy stores, especially necessary in endurance running. Trained runners have glycogen levels of up to three times those of untrained persons. This results both from training (70%) and the high-carbohydrate diet which athletes tend to follow (20% to 30% of the improvement).

Increase in the rate of fat oxidation

Fat oxidation is the process by which body fat is used as an energy source. Training increases the rate at which this process occur, and it does so in two ways. Firstly, training increases the enzyme content of muscle cells; these enzymes are responsible for changing food energy into the energy 'currency' that the body needs. Secondly, training also increases the number of blood capillaries surrounding muscle fibres, and which transport oxygen and fuel to the muscle cells. This is advantageous because the enzymes, stored in cell structures called mitochondria, function only in the presence of an adequate oxygen supply, and the efficiency of their functioning is enhanced by increasing the rate at which both oxygen and the fuels in the bloodstream are provided to them.

Shift in the lactate turnpoint

The lactate turnpoint refers to the exercise intensity or running speed at which the concentration of lactate in the blood begins to rise noticeably. Lactate is produced as glycogen is broken down, and its rate of production increases as the intensity of exercise increases. Lactate has been mistakenly labelled as a prime cause of muscle cramps, fatigue and post-race soreness. In fact, lactate may be one of the body's most important substances, as it is a by-product of a process which aims to prevent the muscles becoming acidic too quickly, and therefore fatiguing too rapidly. What is more, there is a theory that lactate may be used as an important fuel, released by inactive muscles, to be used by the active muscles. In this way, the body's carbohydrate reserves can be shuttled around the body to areas of greatest need. For example, glycogen stored in the runner's arm muscles is released as lactate during exercise, and transported to the leg muscles where it is burned as an important fuel.

While the idea that there is a precise point during exercise at which the rate of lactate production increases sharply is now in question (and with it the term 'lactate turnpoint'), in the absence of a recognized alternative term, it is useful to use 'lactate turnpoint' to refer to the exercise intensity at which blood lactate concentrations begin to rise dramatically. It is this point which can be shifted to a higher running speed through training. In other words, a runner who undergoes training will be able to exercise at a higher level of

Elite runners such as Shadrack Hoff and Simon Morolong invariably have low percentages of body fat. Training increases the rate at which body fat is used as a source of energy

intensity before significant increases in blood lactate levels becomes noticeable.

The physiology of lactate production and consumption, and its role in endurance running is relatively complex. For a more comprehensive discussion, we refer you to *Lore of Running*.

High-distance training

Studies have indicated that training as much as 120 km per week does not increase the intensity of effort you are able to sustain during marathons, i.e., your fatigue resistance. Extra training, it seems, improves running efficiency, thus enabling you to run faster for the same amount of effort. It could be that the sole physiological benefit of very high weekly training distances is an increase in running efficiency.

Perhaps the important point to remember is that there have been relatively few scientific studies to determine the effects of high mileage, or indeed any form of specific training, on running performance. Rather, most studies have concentrated on the physiological changes that result from training. However, the link between specific physiological changes and improved performance are assumed, rather than proven.

Until more specific studies have been performed, we must be cautious in the interpretation of these physiological findings. Training which does not cause measurable physiological changes could be beneficial in ways still not fully understood.

PSYCHOLOGY: control of the mind

We have already noted that physiological advantages are, to a large extent, genetically acquired. We have also seen that regular exercise (training) plays an important role in optimizing performance within the limits of our genetic make-up. Nevertheless, many athletes who have reached exceptional heights in their careers, strongly believe that psychological rather than physiological factors ultimately separate the elite from the lesser runners. Former world record holders Roger Bannister, Herb Elliott and Derek Clayton, as well as the 1994 world half-marathon champion, Elana Meyer, all believe this to be the case.

The role of the mind

The mind is most certainly a powerful conditioner, feeding our bodies with certain performance-inhibiting and performance-enhancing information. The fact that elite athletes condition themselves to run just fast enough to win a gold medal, or to better records by the narrowest of margins, testifies to the power of the mind as the ultimate controlling force. It makes little sense to run 30 seconds faster than the opposition if the rewards (conscious and sub-conscious) are similar if you do so by one second or one metre – the distance by which Alberto Salazar won the 1982 Boston Marathon. One's limits are thus defined by the performance of the opposition, or by existing records, and it is the mind which tunes performance to these marks, enabling the athlete to achieve greatness by a mere fraction.

Alberto Salazar, shown here running in the 1994 Comrades, is an example of an athlete whose harnessing of mental resources has had exceptional results

It has been said that champions telescope into their relatively short racing careers all the achievements of the champions of the past and then stop with a gold medal, just as their predecessors did. Since their targets are set in the form of medals and existing records, rather than speed, the winning speed cannot be considered to be the product of ultimate physiological limits. This conclusion applies to lesser runners as well. It could be that we erect mental barriers that are short of our ultimate physiological limitations. Thus, the 2:30 barrier for the standard marathon is really an artificial limit to be reached, as is the three or four hour barrier. In other words, we fall far short of our true potential because we have yet to expose ourselves to the full power of our minds.

According to the 1500 m record holder, Herb Elliott: 'There's probably going to be a quantum leap forward when we understand our minds better. I believe we just barely understand our psychological capabilities at this stage of the game....'

Belief system

Belief in ourselves is a crucial determining factor in all sports, and indeed in many facets of life. Former South African marathon and track champion, Ewald Bonzet, now a leading coach, claims that from a physiological point of view, Ricky Robinson (Western Province sub-four minute miler of the 1980s) should never have run the mile faster than four minutes. Yet Robinson's mental strength was such that he accomplished this feat on more than one occasion.

Performance is a function of the athlete's belief system: an inbuilt programme, moulded by life's experiences and influences, which interprets incoming stimuli and formulates an appropriate response. Many athletes perform to a standard below their potential because their belief system is programmed for that particular standard. What is required is a reprogramming of their belief system. This is discussed in more detail in Chapter 7.

There is a strong relationship between a positive belief system and a winning response. In a competitive situation, when we are faced with a challenge – be it in a race for line honours or in a personal duel with a clubmate or work colleague – it is our belief system which ultimately determines our response. This challenge becomes particularly apparent towards the end of the race when the physical capabilities of competitors are essentially the same; it is mental toughness that will determine the victor.

Other factors

In addition to a positive belief system, superior performance demands that we control our thoughts and emotions, particularly our levels of anxiety and arousal.

Thus, for those who wish to run their best, training the mind becomes as important (arguably even more so) as training the body. In Chapter 7 we focus more closely on how this can be achieved, and also look at some of the psychological highs and lows associated with running.

Ricky Robinson's strong mental qualities have not only made him an exceptionally tough competitor, they have enabled him to overcome apparent physiological limitations

II

TRAINING

4 TRAINING THE BODY:
21 Principles of
running your best

Training, Franz Stampfl once remarked, is principally an act of faith. Stampfl, coach to the world's first sub-four minute miler, Roger Bannister, undoubtedly employed the best-known scientific training techniques of the time to condition Bannister to achieve the mark. Equally certain is the fact that Stampfl did not believe that faith alone would work athletic wonders on the track. He was merely acknowledging, wisely, that his ideas were unlikely to be the last word on training, his methods not necessarily the best for all athletes for all time.

Shortly after she broke the world 15 km road record in November 1991 (46:57), Elana Meyer echoed Stampfl's observation when she commented that it probably didn't matter what you did in training, within reason, as long as you believed in your specific training programme.

If you bought this book in the hope of discovering a running panacea which would supply a magic formula for every need, circumstance and distance, you will be disappointed. However much you may want to believe that there is one ideal training programme which will enable you to reach your ultimate athletics goals, if only you can find it, no such programme exists. There are in fact a variety of programmes and principles which, if pursued with the necessary motivation and belief, will significantly improve your performance.

On the other hand, the history of athletic and scientific research has taught us that there are certain advantageous principles which should be followed as well as pitfalls to be avoided if you wish to optimize your running performance. It is to these that we now turn.

Fifteen training rules were discussed in *Lore of Running*. These, we believe, form the basis of a sound approach to training. We have modified these rules and added to them in the light of further experience and knowledge, and we present here the twenty-one Principles for Running Your Best. These can be regarded as the "rites of passage" for any runner wishing to come of age.

We acknowledge the insights of some of South Africa's top distance running coaches in helping us to compile both this list and the included training programmes (see Appendix 2, pp. 215-27). Those who contributed are (some of the better-known athletes whom they have coached are indicated in brackets): Andrew Bell (Evelinah Tshabalala, Jean Rayner), Ewald Bonzet (Marius-Hugo Schlechter, Tanya Peckham, Ron Boreham), George Bradley (Deon Fouche, Helleen Joubert, Gert de Bruyn), Darren de Reuck (Colleen de Reuck), Bruce Fordyce (himself), Klasie Geldenhuys (Xolile Yawa, Thabiso Moqali, Simon Meli), Pieter Labuschagne (Elana Meyer, Zola Budd-Pieterse), Bobby McGee (Johan Landsman, Isaac Opperman, Colleen de Reuck, Jantjie Marthinus) and Richard Turnbull (Mathews Temane, Willie Mtolo, Warren Petterson).

PRINCIPLE 1:
Constantly re-evaluate your condition, progress and races, and set achievable (new) goals

The need for the application of this principle is so obvious that it is often overlooked. Our ideal training programme, if it exists, is 'ideal' only for as long as our circumstances remain constant. As they are unlikely to do so (we age, have children, take up new jobs, experience changes in health, and so forth), we need to ask ourselves at regular intervals whether we are still on course for our intermediate and longer term goals. Be realistic. Nothing is as demotivating as goals that are clearly out of reach, and it is far better to re-define those goals (or chart a new course, if necessary) in the light of our changed circumstances. Illness, injury, new family or job circumstances, and pregnancy are just some of the reasons for re-evaluation. Obviously this principle also holds for those changes in our lifestyle which may enable us to aim higher, for example, recovery from illness or injury.

Implicit in this principle is the need to evaluate yourself honestly (both physically and mentally) at the outset of your

Elana Meyer, South Africa's best-known athlete of the 1990s. Her gradual and consistent improvement over the last ten years is a model for impatient would-be champions

running career, or when you resume running after an extensive break from the sport. Ask yourself:

- How badly do I want to achieve this goal?
- How can I improve my self-discipline?
- What is my state of health?
- What are my current ambitions?
- What inbuilt or external limitations exist to hinder my progress? (Here it will be useful to refer to Principle 21: understand limitations of age and gender.)

Bear in mind that at least to begin with, running is neither easy nor enjoyable. You will need great motivation and discipline to survive the first few months before running becomes habitual and pleasurable.

For your convenience, we have included an outline of a framework within which you can set targets for your next year's running programme (see Appendix 3, p. 239).

PRINCIPLE 2:
Do the minimum amount of training to achieve your goal

Far from being the 'cop-out' that this may first appear, this principle is designed to allow us to achieve our best times in those races which we rate as the most important, and to maintain our enthusiasm for the sport.

You may be aware of those who excel during training, but who seem to leave their best form behind when it comes to racing. Their race results simply do not reflect the enormous effort they invested in training for the event.

Others, however, appear to do far less during the training period, but nevertheless produce impressive results on race day. Mark Plaatjes' victory in the 1991 Los Angeles Marathon was a classic example. At a pre-race news conference, his main rivals boasted of the substantial weekly mileages which they had logged in the build-up to the race. Plaatjes, a former University of the Witwatersrand physiotherapy graduate and subsequent winner of the marathon at the 1993 World Athletics Championships in Stuttgart, stated in contrast that he had moved away from the high mileage approach that the Americans favoured, and had returned to the low volume–high intensity programme he had followed in South Africa. Plaatjes went on to win the marathon in 2:10:29 – at that stage, the fastest time by an American resident for several years.

Similarly, when five-times Hawaiian Ironman winner Paula Newby-Fraser first left South Africa for the United States in order to compete as a professional triathlete, she fell into the 'distance trap'. She reduced the intensity of her training and upped the duration. Her performances deteriorated. She later returned to the same high intensity (and lower volume) training programme she had followed in South Africa, and her incredible run of success commenced. Later she would write: 'I did it on less'.

The victories of Plaatjes and Newby-Fraser, however, were not achieved by minimal training, but rather by a wise combination of training for speed and distance (see Principle 9), while forsaking the high mileage approach. What we are advocating here is a cautious approach in terms of distance and speed, both when starting out, and later when your goals have become more ambitious. It is always better, physically and psychologically, to err on the side of

Wits physiotherapy student Mark Plaatjes dominated cross-country running in South Africa in 1985. Here he is congratulated by Mathews Temane after his championship title

The Argus

undertraining. (When in doubt, do less, according to Bruce Fordyce).

For some reason, part of the 'macho' mythology of running is that top runners achieve greatness by enduring training programmes quite beyond the level of the rest of us. The best runners, the world would have us believe, are those who train the hardest. But it is clear that genetic ability has more to do with why the great athletes beat us than their supposedly more rigorous training programmes, and there is no earthly way that training can reduce the gap that divides us from them. Unfortunately, many runners simply will not accept this, and continue in the fallacious belief that all they have do to run very well is to train very hard. They end up doing far too much in order to try to compensate for their genetic shortcomings, and this invariably leads to staleness and injury.

Another reason why the 'do the minimum' adage makes sense, particularly for beginners, is that we now appreciate that bones, tendons and muscles are simply not able to adapt overnight to the cumulative stress of regular training. For this reason, initial goals should be conservative, and it is best to begin training with a period of walking and possibly slow jogging. Our suggested training programme for beginners (see Appendix 2, p. 215) incorporates just such an initial walking period.

In addition, adhering to a conservative programme is likely to enable you to retain enthusiasm for and commitment to your running goals, whereas failing to maintain a more ambitious one could lead to early retirement from the sport, either due to injury or disillusionment. Principles 8 and 9 are also important in this respect.

An obvious question arises from the 'do the minimum' principle: how do I know what the minimum is? And how can I monitor my training to ensure an optimal workload? This is discussed under the next principle, which is a corollary to this one.

PRINCIPLE 3:
Beware of the Greedy Runner Syndrome

The central principle on which all training operates is that of 'progressive overload'. In order to improve our ability to run faster or further, we must subject our body to increasing levels of stress in the form of workload. By adapting to each new stress, our bodies become stronger or faster until we are able to reach our chosen goal. The secret is to know the optimal level of stress to place on our bodies. Too little, and we will not adapt sufficiently to meet our target. Too much, and we will soon become demotivated, disillusioned and probably injured ex-runners. The third Principle for running your best is aimed at addressing the latter error.

Consider the following scenarios:
- You have just watched Josiah Thugwane winning the Olympic Marathon title on television, and feel motivated to take up the sport in order to complete a marathon;
- You have completed 10 km for the first time and the exhilaration of doing so has made you determined to tackle the half marathon or run 10 km in a much faster time;

- You have just run your first sub-three hour marathon and have now set your sights on 2 hours 50 minutes;
- A personal best for the 56 km Two Oceans makes you determined to achieve a further personal best in the 89 km Comrades Marathon six weeks later;
- You have excelled at a provincial championship event and have been chosen to represent your province for the first time at the national championships a month later;
- You have just set a world-class track time; the media are now tipping you for an Olympic medal.

All the above stimuli can be harnessed in a positive way to enable us to achieve new heights in our sport, but they carry a hidden danger which, if not recognized, could result in our falling prey to the Greedy Runner Syndrome. The danger lies in the fact that the euphoria of success can blind us into believing the biggest lie in distance running: if I have achieved this performance on my current training programme, surely I can improve significantly if I train twice as hard. There are almost as many examples as there are runners to prove that this is not true.

More often than not, this psychologically-induced sudden increase in training load has the reverse effect, leading to sub-standard performance, illness and injury. We must thus ensure that the demands we place on ourselves in training are in accordance with our level of development, and that they reflect optimal rather than maximal stress. A session of 20 interval repetitions over 400 m with 30 second recovery jogs between each repetition would not, for example, be appropriate for an athlete who has recently run 5 km for the first time.

Training load

How can we ensure that our training load is optimal? Firstly, by following a balanced approach to training in accordance with the 21 Principles for Running Your Best (particularly Principles 7 to 13); and secondly, by finding a reliable system which can monitor whether our bodies are adapting to training loads in a constructive or destructive way. Monitoring can be done either by making subjective assessments of the intensity of our effort, both during and after training, or by monitoring our heart rate during exercise.

Subjective assessments

There are several ways in which you can assess the effectiveness of your training programme:

- During exercise: a useful 'on-the-run' means of assessment
  is whether the residual leg-weariness which often accompanies training, vanishes or grows worse as you progress
  on your training run. If the latter, this is a serious warning
  that your body is over-stressed and probably overtrained
  (see below), and that further high-intensity training will be
  counter-productive until total recovery is achieved.
- Post-exercise: there is a close relationship between your
  exercising heart rate, which is directly related to the intensity of your exercise, and how you actually perceive the
  effort you are making. By regularly recording your perceived effort during training sessions in a log book (say on
  a scale of 1 to 10) and noting your heart rates during exercise, as well as your recovery from these sessions, you will
  build up a record of valuable information which you
  should be able to use to prevent yourself from straying into
  'Greedy Runner' territory.
- Two days later: you should recover from any session within
  a maximum of 48 hours. If not, you have trained too heavily and need to be on your guard against overtraining.

*Running places
stress on
bones, muscles
and tendons.
Unless
beginners and
those returning
to the sport
after a long
break follow a
programme
which
gradually
builds fitness,
injuries are
bound to
happen*

Colleen de Reuck (left) and Frith van der Merwe are both top athletes who have experienced the pitfalls of overtraining

Monitoring of heart rate

An important method for determining effort during running is to monitor heart rate during exercise. We know that maximum heart rate falls with increasing age. A simple equation to remember is that the maximum heart rate (in beats per minute) can be estimated as 220 minus age in years. So, for example, the maximum heart rate at 40 is 180 beats per minute and, following the training rule outlined in Principle 10, most of your training at the age of 40 should be done with your heart rate between 108 and 162 beats per minute (60-90% of 180). Please note that these figures are not to be regarded as absolute givens, as the maximum heart rate varies widely and is not always accurately predicted by this equation. The following equations are considered to be more accurate:

Men: MHR (Maximum Heart Rate) = 214 minus (0,8 x age)
Women: MHR = 209 minus (0,7 x age).

These formulas, however, can also be liable to error, and the best way to determine your individual maximum heart rate is to run 1-2 km at maximum effort. The highest heart rate achieved this way is your maximum heart rate.

To use this method to control exercise intensity, the pulse rate must be measured accurately. This can best be done by using a light-weight heart rate monitor, which is strapped to your chest while you run. However, these monitors are expensive and are unlikely to be accessible to all runners. Your heart rate can also be measured by counting the pulse rate at any convenient spot where you feel a pulse. The most common spot is the artery on the thumb-side of your wrist. Touch this spot lightly with three fingers until a pulse is felt. Start counting immediately after exercise and count for 10 seconds only, as the pulse rate rapidly returns to slower resting levels. Then multiply the 10-second count by six to calculate a heart rate in beats per minute.

Part of the value of heart-rate monitoring is that it can identify a state of early overtraining. If the heart rate is abnormally elevated, i.e., higher than normal either at rest or when running at a specific speed, then the body is over-tired and needs more rest, not more training.

Overtraining: end product of the Greedy Runner Syndrome

The Greedy Runner Syndrome manifests itself in various forms. One form is the failure to incorporate adequate periods of rest into the training schedule (see Principle 8). Another common symptom is impatience, often demonstrated by attempting to reap benefits from a peaking programme in the absence of sufficient base preparation (see Principle 14). A third tell-tale sign comes in the form of over-racing.[1]

---

[1] *While regular (often weekly) racing has been used effectively by some athletes to supplement speed training, an uncontrolled and over-ambitious racing programme can be counter-productive, preventing the athlete from performing at their highest peak on the most important race day. This is especially so when the race distance exceeds 15 km. We should also stress here the need to race over progressively longer distances. For example, before attempting a marathon, you should gain reasonable experience in races up to the half marathon and then up to 32 km. Unfortunately, in South Africa, the lure of the Comrades Marathon has tempted many athletes into taking short cuts in their training in order to be able to race the 90 km distance at the end of May, when the Comrades is held. Frith van der Merwe is an example of a runner who concentrated first on ultramarathons before gaining her South African colours at 15 km and in the standard marathon. This approach, combined with an excessive ultramarathon racing programme, has possibly been to the detriment of her career.*

A combination of these three running vices can lead to one of the most feared maladies of the distance runner: overtraining. This is the most extreme form of the Greedy Runner Syndrome.

Symptoms

The diagnosis of overtraining is often made after an athlete has failed to recover from training-induced stress within a reasonable period. This staleness, from which it can take weeks to recover, is characterized by physical and emotional behavioral changes. Impaired performance, gradual weight loss, increase in waking heart rate of more than five beats per minute, heavy legs, persistent muscle soreness, susceptibility to infection and the swelling of lymph glands, and an increased fluid intake at night are some examples of the physical symptoms that can develop. Loss of enthusiasm and drive, lethargy, inability to concentrate at work, irritability, loss of appetite, and loss of libido are the chief emotional symptoms of overtraining.

Causes

Failure to recognize our symptoms at an early stage is often due to an ingrained belief that runners tend to hold: that the only cure for inadequate performance is to train harder. So we do exactly this, only to find that our performances worsen still further. Our response is to train even harder, until we eventually reach a stage where we are physically incapable of training.

We must also remember that while training or racing too much is the usual recipe for overtraining, there are other non-running factors which can predispose to overtraining. These include poor nutrition, lack of sleep, adverse weather conditions, work pressures, emotional conflict, monotonous training, and general living stress.

Ewald Bonzet (right) has been one of South Africa's most versatile athletes; he has excelled over distances ranging from 1 500 m to the marathon. Also a successful coach, here he races to victory in tandem with one of his 'charges', Marius-Hugo Schlechter

Prevention

Essential in order to avoid overtraining is an awareness of the different stages of this syndrome, and the ability to differentiate between the general fatigue which accompanies normal training, and the slightly increased fatigue which indicates overtraining. Documenting your training in a diary (especially details of your heart rate) will enable you to detect signs of overtraining at an early stage, and so take action to avoid becoming a victim of full-blown overtraining. Time trials can be particularly useful. As long as your weekly performance over a set trial distance (say 5 km) is improving for the same effort, or your recovery period is shortening following the same performance level, you are not overtraining. Once you have to run harder to achieve the same time, overtraining has occurred.

Similarly, if your heart rate or perception of effort is either the same or lower at the same or a faster running speed during your time trial, then you are not overtraining.

Running in scenic surroundings is an ideal way to recover (both mentally and physically) from a high intensity training run or race. Alternately, do it just for the pleasure of it

An alternative and perhaps preferable way to assess whether you are overtraining, is to run these time trials at the same heart rate, and to monitor one's fitness by one's finishing time. Provided that your times improve with training, you are becoming fitter without overtraining yourself.

Treatment

If you fail to identify early indicators and maintain your hard training schedule, you are likely to suffer what Bruce Fordyce has termed 'the plods' (sore muscles, a sluggish feeling of general fatigue and possibly diarrhoea). These symptoms will disappear within 48 hours if you rest. If you continue to train hard in spite of these symptoms, you are in danger of crashing into the full-blown overtrained state. In this case, recovery could take up to two months, during which no hard training should take place.

The only effective treatment for severe overtraining, which has been linked to persistent muscle damage and which is probably the protective response of an exhausted body, is to rest (or at most, do a little light jogging) until the desire to run returns. The lesson to learn is that we must be sensitive to messages from our body, which is the theme of the fourth Principle of Running Your Best.

PRINCIPLE 4:
Your training schedule is always subservient to what your body tells you

'I remember talking to John Walker, former world record holder in the mile, about his training. He let his body dictate his schedule. For instance, if he planned to run 10 hard quarters for an evening workout and felt terrible after running one, he would pack up and go home. I thought that was great. I could never do that. If I planned 15, I ran 15.' (Derek Clayton, 1981).

The Australian marathoner Derek Clayton, the first man to break the 2:09 barrier in the standard marathon, was known for his remarkably high mileage training weeks. He also suffered several setbacks through injury, which eventually cut his career short. Could he have achieved even higher standards if he had learnt to listen to his body?

We have already seen the importance of monitoring or listening to our bodies to avoid succumbing to the Greedy Runner Syndrome. Whether we monitor our heart rates or assess ourselves by using the subjective method, the bottom line is that programme schedules should be followed only as far as our bodies are able to adapt in a positive way to the training load placed upon them. This is absolutely vital. Injury and illness apart, training programmes take no account of the variety of external factors affecting our lives: work, family, emotional strain, travel, etc. While most runners are prepared to concede a training day or two to injury or illness, many fail to adapt their training load to other external circumstances, and their performances suffer as a result.

Not only will we fail to benefit from training if our bodies are not able to cope with the increased load, but our condition is likely to deteriorate. Inappropriate training performed with sore or damaged muscles will not only be ineffectual (obviously damaged muscles are unable to perform properly), but will also delay muscle and whole body recovery.

In addition, studies have indicated that while moderately trained runners have more resilient immune systems, highly trained athletes may be more vulnerable to intercurrent infection such as colds and 'flu. Fulfilling your pre-planned training commitments for the day when your body is pleading for rest could lead to illness.

There is merit, however, in following a structured programme. Especially for novice runners, who need to overcome the effects of 'running inertia' experienced by most when getting started in the sport, the advantages of adhering doggedly to a fixed routine may outweigh the disadvantages. Yet in the end, the ability to gauge how much training to do on any particular day (the 'artistic' side of running your best: see Principle 18) ultimately determines running success, and will assist you in your quest to run your best.

PRINCIPLE 5:
Vary your training as much as possible

There is more to beginner's luck than just luck! Apart from the benefit of not having had sufficient time to develop bad habits or psychological barriers, the enthusiasm and vigour of a new convert can often prevail against the experienced and better practised campaigner. This was clearly apparent during South Africa's participation for the first time in the Cricket World Cup in Australia in 1992/93, where the South African side defeated teams which were considered superior in terms of ability and experience.

Even a strenuous session should provide variety. Here two athletes tackle a change of terrain – a steep grassy slope

Whereas an enthusiastic running novice is unlikely to ever defeat a highly trained athlete of similar genetic potential, the benefits of novelty can be harnessed within our training programmes through the incorporation of variety into our type of training, intensity of training, structure of sessions, chosen routes, terrain on which we run, and training companions. By keeping a balance in our programmes through the incorporation of variety in their functioning, we will also be following Principle 20: understand the concept of holism.

Because the mind (as we have seen in Chapter 3 and explore more fully in Chapter 7) is such a powerful controller, it is important to avoid boredom in training. Always try to structure your session, no matter how strenuous, so that it can provide a degree of mental stimulation, and the results will be readily apparent.

Strangely enough, many runners appear unable or unwilling to experiment with new sessions, methods and training routes, preferring to adhere to tried and tested (although not necessarily optimum) formulae. Variety is essential. The harder the work programme, the more important it is to introduce new ideas and new ways of achieving them.

It should be noted, however, that variety does not imply non-specificity. It is important that our training sessions should be as specific as possible and this is the essence of the next principle.

PRINCIPLE 6:
Every session should have a specific function

All training is specific to the exercise type, and there is little 'cross-over' of the training effects. Running trains only the legs, leaving the upper body relatively untrained, whereas canoeing and swimming chiefly train the upper body, leaving the legs untrained.

Does this mean that cross-training, such as cycling, canoeing, swimming and gym work, is a waste of time in our endeavours to run our best? Not at all. It is important that this principle is read in conjunction with Principle 20: understand the concept of holism. Because running is a multifaceted function including, for example, muscle propulsion, cardiovascular functioning and mental processes, an optimal training programme should relate to each of these components – in other words, it should operate on the principle of holism. But to be effective, training should nevertheless recognize an end-goal and be directed primarily at that goal – the principle of specificity. Your training for a mountain race, for example, will be different to that for a 1500 m race on the track.

Cycling, canoeing and swimming are ineffective in developing more powerful or efficient leg muscles; but will nonetheless stress your cardiovascular system and your metabolism, thus improving both. These disciplines may be less effective than running in doing so, but they play an important role if you have applied adequate or excessive stress to your muscular-skeletal system, but still wish to stress your cardiovascular and metabolic systems.

German ultra-distance runner Charly Doll, who won the 1993 Comrades Marathon, included substantial amounts of cross-country skiing into a programme which already incorporated high-volume running, thus maximizing the training of his cardiovascular and metabolic systems while remaining injury-free (by reducing his amount of weight-bearing activity). Gym work can be highly effective in applying specific stress to particular muscle-groups (for example, in strengthening your quadriceps for downhill running).

Ideally, elite athletes should be able to identify precisely which body functions and muscle groups are used in their event, and to what extent, and devise specific training routines to apply optimal (and probably individual) stress to those functions and groups. Most of us, however, have limited time, and before we concern ourselves with the marginal benefits of cross-training, we should ensure that we apply ourselves to the activity which will be of the most all-round benefit to our endeavours to run our best – running itself.

The essential practical point is that the closer you tailor your training to the specific demands of the sport for which you are training, and to the environment in which you are expecting to compete, the better you will perform. We have previously described the benefits of adapting to the particular circumstances in which you expect to be racing,

Cycling provides useful supplementary training for runners, stressing the cardio-vascular system while giving weight-bearing muscles a break

Cross-country specialists had the edge over faster track athletes at the 1993 World Championships. Ireland's Catherina McKiernan (moving up behind Zola Budd-Pieterse) went on to take the silver medal behind Albertina Dias, another cross-country ace

whether at high altitude, in warm weather or over hilly terrain. To train at the coast for an altitude event, in cool conditions for warm-weather competition, or on flat terrain for a race over hills, would be to run the risk of being unfit for your particular race, no matter how hard or long you have trained. You are equally in danger of racing on undertrained muscle fibres if you train exclusively at a slow pace (see Principles 9 and 10).

At the World Cross-country Championships in Spain in 1993, Albertina Dias and Catherina McKiernan finished first and second in the women's senior event, beating several more favoured (and faster) athletes, among them the American Lyn Jennings and South Africa's Elana Meyer. An important factor was that the successful pair were specifically fit for cross-country running, having raced regularly on the world circuit leading up to the championships. In other words, they had specifically trained the muscles which come into play during running on a twisting course over uneven terrain. Jennings and Meyer, on the other hand, had chosen a track and road build-up in order to concentrate on their speed, but in the process they may have compromised on specific cross-country fitness.

Similarly, it can be predicted that the gold medallists in the distance events (most especially the marathon) in the 1996 Olympic Games in Atlanta, Georgia, will be those who either come from or who have trained in hot, humid conditions, similar to those that will prevail in Atlanta in August. The fittest athletes will win those races only if they are equally well-acclimatized to running in hot weather.

PRINCIPLE 7:
Plan medium- and long-term programmes which incorporate specific, but non-exclusive phases

An important tenet of this principle is to train consistently for most of the year. Programmes should preferably be based on a commitment to train for at least ten months of the year. Where possible, this should involve running six days a week. Elite athletes should aim to train for eleven months. Training consistently, however, does not mean that you should train at a similar intensity for ten or eleven months. This would be a recipe for disaster, and would be likely to lead either to breakdown through injury or illness if the intensity was too high, or to under-achieving in your race aspirations because the intensity was too low. What then should be our approach?

Periodization

The concept of periodization in training is embraced by many leading coaches, and is a concept we endorse. It is, however, often misunderstood. Periodization is the basis of Principle 7, and simply means dividing up a longer term programme (say a year) into shorter phases or periods (between 4 to 12 weeks), which in turn can be divided into sub-phases (1 to 3 weeks), and even further into weekly and daily sessions. Each phase and sub-phase is aimed at achieving a certain result which will contribute to a final goal, usually that of completing a race in a certain time. Periodization, or a programme broken into phases, should essentially be based on an understanding of the principle of base training and peaking, and this is clearly spelt out in Principle 14. It should also accommodate sufficient periods of rest (Principle 8), without which athletes will be unable to reach their potential.

Elana Meyer and her support system! Coach Pieter Labuschagne (left), husband Michael, and former agent Bernard Rose have been integral to her success. Labuschagne's emphasis on the correct application of rest when training has been valuable in preparing Meyer for major events

While the elements of the programme will vary according to each individual, it is essentially made up of base training (generally easy aerobic running of consistent pace), conditioning (specific race preparation), and recuperation phases, as illustrated in Figure 4.1 (p. 95). It is extraordinary how many runners, aspiring to run their best, never progress past base training. They reach a plateau beyond which they seem unable to move.

The conditioning phase (Figure 4.1) consists of sub-phases, each of which emphasize one specific aspect of conditioning (such as endurance, power or speed), without ignoring other aspects. Each sub-phase should be followed by a period of active rest, where the emphasis is on easy aerobic running, rhythmic striding, stretching, and possibly cross-training. The training schedules given in Tables 3 and 4 in Appendix B are based on these principles.

Incidentally, what we have labelled 'power' is commonly and colloquially referred to as 'strength'. In fact, the 'strength' phase of training has more to do with conditioning the muscles for power (the rate of work done) than with building muscle strength itself.

Many coaches, particularly those of longer distance road athletes, apply the base-conditioning-recuperation cycle over relatively long periods, with their athletes undergoing at the most three conditioning phases in one year, each lasting six to 12 weeks. Others (including Pieter Labuschagne, who has coached Zola Budd-Pieterse and Elana Meyer) apply it over much shorter periods.

Labuschagne bases his strategy on a four-week cycle, the first two weeks of which consist of aerobic base running with an emphasis on endurance, the third on active rest, and the fourth on high-quality race-specific training.

A typical phased approach to race preparation (marathons in particular) would incorporate endurance, power and speed phases after several months of aerobic base running. The length of these phases varies, but would be in the region of two to four weeks respectively, depending on the preferences of coaches, as well as the individual requirements of athletes. These phases would be followed by a one to three week-taper, in which the training volume would be reduced (see Principle 14).

Further discussion of the implications of the methods employed during individual sessions, such as fartlek, hillwork, intervals, and time trials, are described in Appendix B (see pp. 220-4.) We note here in passing, however, the importance of hills in the training schedule of the distance runner. If you lack the time to commit yourself to a variety of high-intensity training sessions, make sure that you incorporate regular hillwork sessions in your programme. Hillwork builds aerobic efficiency and muscle power, and stresses most of the running-related body components. It is the all-in-one workout which, better than any other, will give you an assured return on your investment.

PRINCIPLE 8:
Incorporate recovery periods in regular cycles

One of the most important, but most neglected, aspects of training is the correct application of rest. Pieter Labuschagne rates the correct application of rest as the most important principle in his approach to coaching, while other top coaches, including George Bradley and Bobby McGee, have found that it is impossible for athletes to improve without appropriate structuring of rest in their programmes.

Disciplined and structured hill work is a core element in training to run your best

No runner can endure uninterrupted sessions of high-intensity training for days on end. A session of intense training should be followed by one which allows for recovery. The same applies to a high-intensity week (two or more hard sessions) and even a hard year. If, for example, you have set several personal best times over varying distances and surpassed your goals at the Two Oceans and Comrades Marathons all in the same year, you might do well to ease up the following year before planning a renewed assault on your records. This is especially important for Comrades runners. We note that few runners do well in consecutive Comrades Marathons; a good race is often followed by a poor race the following year. In our view, this is because the bodies of most runners take more than a year to recover from a hard Comrades Marathon. The obvious exception is Bruce Fordyce, who was able to run well in consecutive Comrades Marathons for more than a decade. However, he is a unique, perhaps never-to-be-repeated exception who in fact proves the rule.

Unfortunately, human greed and impatience interfere with common sense. We readily dispense this wisdom to others, but are blind to our own failings. Although we can clearly see errors in the programmes of other runners, we find it extremely difficult, especially when we are running well, to accept that it may be time to back off before we risk succumbing to the Greedy Runner Syndrome (Principle 3), which will ultimately be detrimental to our performance, and will possibly even cut short our running careers.

There is no certainty as to why the body is unable to train hard every day, but it is probably due to muscle damage of the same type (but less severity) caused by marathon racing. It is probable that it takes about 24-48 hours to recover from this degree of muscle damage, rather than the six to twelve weeks needed after a 42 km marathon race. However, although superficial recovery may occur within four to twelve weeks, we suggest that the cumulative effects of racing marathons are such that you should not consider racing more than two per year, and preferably only one. In addition, there may be a central or brain component to this delayed process of recovery. The example of Alberto Salazar, whose recovery from what seemed to be a severe overtraining syndrome was prompted by his use of a centrally-acting medication (Prozac), has been described in Chapter 1.

Wise runners must learn that if their previous training session was hard, regardless of what their mind tells them, or what they imagine their competitors are doing in training, they must allow their bodies periods of recovery to restock their energy stores and to repair the micro-damage caused by the previous day's heavy training. Hard training when the body is not fully recovered simply compounds damage already done.

This lesson is essential when planning racing strategy. It is not possible to race your best if your muscles have not fully recovered from training sessions and it is therefore essential to undergo a 'tapering' period of lower volume (although possibly high-intensity) running during the period leading up to an important race. This taper is described in more detail under Principle 15, and also in Chapter 9 (p. 177).

How much intensive training can our bodies stand? This is something that runners will have to determine for themselves. Your success will largely depend on whether or not you achieve an appropriate balance. A rule of thumb which appears to apply to the 'average' runner, is that when training hard, three moderately hard or two highly intensive sessions a week are optimum, but only for six to ten weeks at a time.

Circumstantial rest

Apart from formally including recovery sessions in our training programmes, we should also be prepared to incorporate rest or recovery periods on an ad hoc basis whenever our non-running circumstances dictate. This echoes Principles 4 and 20. We cannot expect to respond positively to a scheduled strenuous work-out while experiencing stressful work or home circumstances. Failure to abort such a session in favour of a light aerobic run will prove counterproductive and could lead to enforced prolonged rest due to injury or illness. Methods of assessing when you are bordering on overtraining, and need to incorporate rest in your programme, are described under Principle 3.

Of course, for those of us who struggle to incorporate the odd session of running into a demanding schedule of resting, the rigid application of this principle is unlikely to have profound effects on our running performance!

PRINCIPLE 9:
Train first for stamina, then for speed

The training philosophy pendulum has swung from a near-exclusive emphasis on long, slow distance (LSD) running in the early part of this century, to a more recent preoccupation with fast, high-intensity running. An exclusive focus on either one of these training polarities is detrimental to the cause of athletes seeking to run their best. By concentrating exclusively on the former, you will be racing on undertrained or untrained fast-twitch muscle fibres. An over-emphasis on speed, however, can rapidly lead to physical and mental staleness, illness and injury.

The initial key to successful training is the amount of time you spend running each week, rather than the distance you cover, or the speed at which you run. Therefore, at first, your aim should be to run for a certain time each session. When fresh and rested, you will run further than when you are tired. In this way, the effort will be controlled. Remember that the initial goal in distance training is to gradually increase the

Speed is a vital, but potentially dangerous element of training. Here Melody Marcus (left) and Shadrack Hoff fine-tune their speedwork sessions

speed or effort that can be maintained for prolonged distances. In other words, your initial goal (both if you are a beginner or an experienced runner on the come-back trail) should be to lay a foundation of stamina through LSD, without concerning yourself about speed.

After a few years of stamina-based training (or less in the case of 'come-back' athletes), your performance will eventually reach a definite plateau. To improve further, you must either increase the distance you run in training, or run the same distance, but run some of it at a faster pace; in other words, shift to speed training. For some, excessive weekly training loads in terms of distance are counter-productive, and a more balanced approach, which incorporates a judicious amount of speed training, is advised for most runners.

How does speedwork help? Principle 6 states the specificity of training. In other words, if you train slowly, you are likely to race slowly. Faster running trains the quadriceps muscles, and the fast twitch muscle fibres in all the lower limb muscles. These muscle groups and fibres will be needed during racing, but remain untrained if you only run slowly during training. Speedwork probably increases muscle contractility, increasing the runner's power. Another benefit of speedwork is learning to relax at speed. Furthermore, it is likely that fast running adapts the ventilatory muscles to cope with high work rates, and may help to prevent the occurrence of the 'stitch'.

Speedwork, which should only ever comprise about 10-15% of your total training volume, is also a psychological necessity. Knowing that you have achieved certain training times will equip you mentally to achieve similar or greater goals in racing. Like racing itself, speedwork tests the will and only when you have passed this test, are you ready to race.

Nonetheless, speedwork is not without its risks; the twin dangers are running the sessions too often and too fast. The next Principle elaborates on these dangers.

PRINCIPLE 10:
Train at maximum intensity only for limited periods

Road runners, and marathon athletes in particular, should only train at race pace or faster for 5-15% of their total training distance during the conditioning phase of race preparation. During base training or recovery phases, and during the remaining 85-95% of the conditioning phase, all running should be slower than race pace, and you should feel comfortable enough with your effort level to carry on a conversation with your running companions (the talk test). Should the effort of the run prevent you from talking (except for during a high-intensity session), you are 'straining, not training' and should slow down.

Many of the world's best runners do most of their training at speeds of between 30 and 50 seconds per km slower than their race pace. In simple terms, this means that if you are a novice runner who ultimately plans to run a standard marathon in 4:30:00, you will need to run your marathon at a speed of about 6 minutes per km. This means that your training speed should be between 6,5 and 7 minutes per km.

As indicated under Principle 7, the conditioning phase should typically extend from six to 12 weeks. High intensity training should never last longer than 14 weeks and this period should include at least three recovery weeks. Six weeks may be a more realistic figure for most athletes. Several top coaches believe that in order to obtain maximum benefit (through maximum intensity, and thus close to maximum heart rate) from a quality session, you should be completely rested prior to your work-out. This can only be achieved through the correct application of rest or recovery in your programme (easy running at less than 60% of maximum heart rate), according to Principle 8.

Xolile Yawa steps up his pace. Athletes should closely monitor the pace at which they train

Thus two important, but limited, phases in your training programme take place at a low and very high percentage of maximum heart rate respectively. What about the remainder? For healthy runners, maximum benefit is achieved by training at between 60 and 90% of maximum heart rate. Ideally, heart rates should fall between these values for most of the training time; close to 90% during higher quality sessions such as fartlek and hill running, and nearer 60 to 70% during aerobic running.

PRINCIPLE 11:
Don't race when training, and race distances in excess of 15 km infrequently

In Chapter 9, we describe the phenomenon of runners who excel in training, but underachieve in races (see p. 190). If you adhere to Principle 11, this is less likely to happen to you.

We have discussed the dangers of training excessively at maximum intensity (see Principle 10). For the same reasons, racing too often can be harmful rather than helpful. A rule of thumb is that the shorter the race, the more frequently it can be run. Races of up to 15 km can be raced regularly, and many athletes use these events as an essential part of their high-intensity training programme. Races beyond 25 km, however, must be approached with caution, as it appears that racing-induced muscle damage starts to occur during races which are longer than 25 km.

As a general rule, only two to three races longer than 30 km should be raced at maximum effort each year. For marathons or ultramarathons, we believe that you should race only one per year at maximum intensity. It is possible that elite athletes are capable of racing only a very limited number of marathons at maximum intensity in their life-time; perhaps as few as three (see Principle 21). If this is so, you should be very cautious in choosing which marathons you want to race. Conservation must be your guiding principle.

You can certainly enter shorter races more frequently, or you can run a greater number of longer races than indicated above, but at sub-maximal effort. The danger is that it is easy to succumb to racing atmosphere, and to turn a disciplined sub-maximal training run into a full-out race. The sight of an 'arch-rival' overtaking you could be enough to wreck the most well-conceived training intentions. The best way to avoid this is to run with a heart monitor (see Principle 3), or take your pulse at regular intervals. Remember, however, that a sub-maximal race must be just that. Running a marathon 60 minutes slower than normal is a sub-maximal effort; running it only ten minutes slower than normal is almost as damaging as racing full-out.

Time trials are an important component in training programmes, but can also be abused. The famous New Zealand coach, Arthur Lydiard advocates regular time trials during the peaking phase: 'Basically they are used to develop coordination in running races over certain distances. Time trials should not be run at full effort, but with strong, even efforts, leaving you with some reserves.'

Lydiard also speaks out strongly against both racing in training and placing too much reliance on the stop-watch. He notes that too much concern with time can cause the athlete to lose confidence, particularly if he or she is tired as a result of heavy training.

A key factor in time trials is that they should be done in the context of a hard training week, and not as part of a taper of any kind (apart from a relatively easy day prior to the time trial as part of the advocated hard day–easy day cycle). This means that you cannot expect to race your best at a time trial. The error that many runners make in running regular time-trials is that they think that each trial must be faster than the last. This is neither desirable nor possible. The surest indication that you are improving is if you are able to run the same or better times in successive time trials, but at a lower heart rate, with less effort, and with a more rapid recovery. Save all-out racing for races.

PRINCIPLE 12:
Never train to exhaustion

High intensity training sessions, which are part of the conditioning phase of your programme, should be run at an effort close to maximum heart rate. These sessions are designed to be strenuous, placing optimal stress on muscle groups, the cardiovascular system and the metabolism. Nonetheless, you should never finish a session feeling as though you are completely unable to run another step at the pace at which you have been training.

To do this would be to risk breaking your body down beyond its ability to recover from the inflicted stress, rather than enabling yourself to adapt to the stress in a positive way, and thus developing the ability to cope with increased loads. Moreover, training to exhaustion inevitably leads to illness or injury.

Apart from the physiological wisdom of abiding by this principle, there are also psychological benefits to be gained. By always holding something back during training, you will enjoy the belief that you have an 'extra gear' to use when racing.

PRINCIPLE 13:
Incorporate aerobic training to maintain or regain enthusiasm

This is a corollary to Principle 8: incorporate recovery periods in regular cycles. Principle 8 recognizes the physiological importance of recovery after strenuous work-outs, to enable your body to recover sufficiently to benefit from the next quality session. Principle 13, however, stresses the mental dimension in training.

We have emphasized the importance of the mind in running your best (see pp. 56–8 and also Chapter 7). Too much quality or high-intensity training has a negative effect on an athlete's motivation. Whereas carefully planned and structured quality sessions can stimulate and encourage, excessive emphasis on speedwork (and excessive could be anything greater than 10 to 15% of your total training volume) can lead to mental staleness. And without the will to complete a block of conditioning training, the battle is lost.

When this occurs, it is essential to cut back on quality sessions and incorporate aerobic running in pleasant surroundings to regain enthusiasm for training. Ideally, you should ensure that even your toughest, highest intensity training months include pleasurable outings including easy aerobic running and variety (see Principle 5). If these 'fun' runs fail to maintain or rekindle your enthusiasm for training, you must consider whether you may have fallen victim to the Greedy Runner syndrome (Principle 3) and take appropriate action.

PRINCIPLE 14:
Understand the principle of peaking

Essentially, peaking is about doing well in the races which are important to you. No runner can race well all the time. The most successful runners are usually those who win the races which are recognized as the most significant. For elite athletes, these races will be national and international championships, with the Olympic Games the ultimate touchstone of success. For average runners, significant races may be any event in which they to attempt to run their best.

Perhaps the best-known examples of peaking are the extraordinary Olympic performances of 'Flying Finn' Lasse Viren. Over a six-year period in the early seventies, Viren seldom looked anything more than average (within the elite context), except in the four races which really mattered – the 5000 m and 10000 m at the 1972 and 1976 Olympic Games. This was because Viren aimed to be in peak condition not once a year, but once every four years. His resulting haul of four gold medals sets him apart as one of the world's great athletes. For Viren, the adage 'the broader the base, the higher the peak' was certainly true. Subsequently, he was to say that the question was not why he did so well in the Olympic Games, but why others did not.

Optimal racing performance occurs only when a period of high-intensity, low-volume (peaking or sharpening) training follows a prolonged build-up period consisting of

The Olympics are the ultimate incentive and peaking target in an elite athlete's career. Two such athletes are Derartu Tulu of Ethiopia and Elana Meyer, whose 10 000 m 'Africa triumph' at the 1992 Olympics captivated millions worldwide

low-intensity, high-volume training (base training). What are the essentials of these two types of training?

Base training

Base training consists mainly of long, slow distance (LSD) running. The aim is to run high mileages without overtraining, and to gradually increase the average speed and distance of the training sessions.

Ideally, base training should continue for at least six months, and preferably one year before any sharpening training begins. You should never feel exhausted after any training session during base training. In fact, the guiding principle is that after any session, you should feel capable of turning around and completing the same workout again.

What are the benefits of base training?
- It develops robust health.
- It conditions the cardiovascular system.
- The slow pace helps to keep injuries to a minimum.
- There is a continuous, slow improvement in performance.
- It has a de-sharpening effect, and stores up 'adaptation energy' – a mysterious substance which has also been described as our 'competitive juice'. This is linked to our ability to maintain drive and enthusiasm for the sport, and our ability to respond to stress in a constructive manner.

Although base training is a very safe training method, it is not without disadvantages. Most significant of these is that base training fails to prepare either the body or the mind for the stresses of racing. In particular, it fails to develop the coordination and the ability to relax at speed that are necessary for peak performance. It also fails to produce those biochemical adaptations that are specific to speed-training; base training alone, therefore, will result in your starting a race on undertrained muscles.

So if you subsist on an exclusive LSD (long, slow distance) running programme, you will probably be able to run forever at a slow pace, and will recover very quickly from even the most demanding performance. However, you will never achieve your full running potential unless you undergo a period of sharpening as well.

Base running has been likened to the laying of the foundations of a building. The taller the building, the stronger the foundations should be. Those impatient souls who wish to reap running rewards as soon as possible and who turn to speedwork before a solid base has been developed, will quickly improve up to a point, but just as quickly fall behind once the short peaking period is at an end.

Sharpening

Sharpening, which we have referred to elsewhere as peaking or the conditioning phase (see Principle 7, for example), consists of any number of different training methods, the common feature of which is that they are all performed at race pace or faster, for varying lengths of time. The most common sharpening techniques are interval running and speed-play (fartlek), hill work, short races, time trials of 1–3 km, and long time trials (tempo runs) of up to 10 km. (These are more fully described in the Training Action Plan in Appendix 2, pp. 220-4.) These sessions become the focal point of training and may be done one to three times weekly, depending on the experience and physical strength of the athlete, and on the intensity of the session.

An important advantage of sharpening is that it teaches you to relax while running at race pace, thereby enabling you to conserve energy even when in 'race mode'. But perhaps the most important benefit of this phase of training is that it produces specific, physiological adaptations that can produce quite dramatic improvements in racing performances. A minute's improvement over 10 km and a huge eleven minute improvement over the marathon have been described as typical responses which can be expected from this programme of sharpening.

This sounds impressive – but be warned that sharpening training has serious potential pitfalls. In particular, it is extremely taxing and uses up 'adaptation energy'; it increases the risk of injury; and, whereas base training builds robust health, sharpening reduces resistance to infection. When sharpening, the athlete is on a knife-edge that divides a peak performance from a disastrous race. For this reason, sharpening can be maintained only for relatively short periods of time, with a probable maximum of between six and 14 weeks. We believe that this rule crosses all human activities, mental or physical. How then, to achieve a peak? Figure 4.1, which is drawn from the experiences of great runners like Viren and New Zealander Peter Snell, compares the performance improvement experienced by runners following two different training methods over a thirty-week period.

Figure 4.1
The theory behind peaking

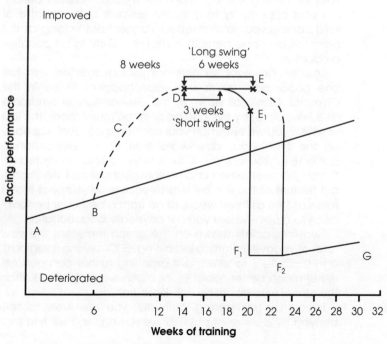

Those runners who choose to do only base training during the thirty-week period can expect to improve their racing performance along the line A-I. Those runners who choose to start sharpening at the six-week point on the graph (point B), so that instead of training only with long, slow distance running, they now include speed training, will find that their racing performance immediately improves quite dramatically. This improvement is shown along the portion B-C-D of the graph. Approximately six to eight weeks after beginning to sharpen (some runners will take longer, others shorter), potential racing performance will reach a plateau (point D).

Certain athletes appear able to improve their condition very quickly, but can maintain their performances only for short periods of time (about three weeks), before they must return to base training. These athletes are able to peak several times during the season. Others, on the other hand, need considerably more training to reach their peak, which they then sustain for much longer (six to eight weeks).

Once you reach your peaking plateau (line D-E in the diagram), you are ready for your best race or series of races (if they are shorter than 30 km); all you need do is maintain your sharpening training. Make the most of this short period. It is your opportunity to reap the rewards of the months of solid training you have invested. Further hard training at this point will be of no benefit; in fact, it is likely to be counterproductive.

Beware, however: runners are seldom satisfied with just one good race, unless that race happens to be in the Olympics. Don't fall victim to the Greedy Runner syndrome (see Principle 3) by trying to pack in too many races, the last of which you will run when your performance level is already on the precipitous downward slide of the performance curve (E-F). You are more than likely to end up injured, ill, thoroughly overtrained and horribly disappointed. An important feature of the line E-F is its steepness. We suspect that it takes as little as three weeks to go from a best-ever performance to a point where you are physically incapacitated.

Two final points shown on the graph represent the slow rate of recovery from overtraining (F-G on the diagram), and the extent to which a sharpening runner can perform either much better (point E), or much worse (point F), than the runner who has done only base training.

If you are sharpening correctly, you are likely to feel buoyed by a sense of physical well-being, and will find that everyday physical activities such as climbing stairs become easier. On the other hand, you are likely to become increasingly sensitive and irritable in everyday situations, and as your body becomes flooded with previously latent energy, you may feel a heightened sexual awareness.

PRINCIPLE 15:
Ensure that you undergo an adequate taper prior to racing

Tapering, or reducing your training volume in the days or weeks prior to your race, has now become accepted running practice. However, this has not always been the standard procedure. Only since the 1960s has tapering become an established science in race preparation, although the term was first coined in 1947. Even today there is uncertainty as to what constitutes the optimal form of tapering. The questions, how intense? for how long? and what form? have not been satisfactorily answered.

Examples abound of record-breaking performances that have resulted after athletes have been forced (through injury or illness) to curtail or stop their training a week or two prior to their race. British athlete Dave Bedford often underachieved, possibly due to an extremely high-volume training load. However, he broke the world 10 000 m track record in 1973, after injuries had resulted in reducing his training load for some months prior to setting the record.

Possibly the most famous example is the case of the Czech Emil Zatopek who, after training intensively, was hospitalized through illness two weeks before the 1950 European Championships. He was discharged just two days prior to the 10 000 m, which he went on to win by a full lap.

Bruce Fordyce tapers for the last three weeks before his ultramarathons and runs very little in the last ten days before the race. His third last week represents about 70% of his maximum weekly volume, his penultimate week 60% and his final week just 25%. This tapering procedure obviously works for him, and his is a basic approach which could be followed in ultra-distance racing.

We suggest a two to three week taper for a standard marathon, and a taper of one to two weeks prior to races of up to 21 km. In our programmes for 10 km and the marathon (Tables 3 and 5 in Appendix 2), we have indicated a two week taper. You should experiment with different lengths

Bruce Fordyce's exceptional ultra-distance performances have stemmed partly from his ability to peak for the races that mattered most, in his case, only one or two ultra-distance races per year

and intensities of tapering until you find a formula which works for you. (See also p. 177 in Chapter 9.)

How should we run during our taper? Until recently, the approach was to reduce both the volume and intensity of training, with many athletes content to do easy jogging the week prior to racing. There is now reason to believe that high-intensity tapers may prove more effective, particularly prior to shorter distance races. Short time trials (500 m to 2 000 m) and interval sessions are recommended, with the latter tapering off in quantity rather than quality (or speed) as the race approaches.

Because of the paucity of literature on tapering, we suggest you experiment with different tapering methods (including absolute rest for up to seven days) to see which is most effective. As a general principle, you should aim to do less than you think you should.

PRINCIPLE 16:
Train more than once per day only after careful evaluation

Some believe that if high-volume training is good, more is better. Principle 3 represents our warning to those who might be tempted to train ever harder and further without careful consideration of the consequences.

Some runners are addicted to reaching a set training distance each week, and, in contravention of Principle 4, will go to extraordinary lengths to hit the magic target. (Remember that this is the cardinal characteristic of the athlete who is great in training; what we want for you is to be great in racing!) One relatively straightforward method of running higher mileages is to train two, or even three times per day.

If your motive for running more than once a day is merely to boost your weekly training kilometre total, we suggest you think again. Particularly if your weekly training mileage is less than 100 km, or if you have been active in the sport for less than three years, you should not consider training more than once a day.

The exception is if your second training session represents cross-training, i.e. does not include additional running. Swimming, cycling or calisthenics, for example, are unlikely to prove detrimental as a second daily training session. By keeping the weight off your legs, these forms of exercise can enhance the metabolic adaptations brought about by training without causing further muscle damage.

Even experienced athletes who are training well over 100 km per week, need to carefully consider the benefits and costs of the extra daily training session. The second session should either be used as a recovery run (for example, the morning after a hard evening session), or should stress different systems or muscle-groups by avoiding weight-bearing activity.

Finally, anyone contemplating training twice a day should consider whether other priorities are being compromised or new stresses added. It's possibly that you might run faster on race day by sleeping an extra hour each night rather than by adding the dawn patrol to the afternoon beat!

PRINCIPLE 17:
Do not underestimate the importance of mental preparation

'Make your mind healthy and it will do the rest,' commented the great distance runner Arthur Newton. Fifty years ago, he recognized that stamina is as much a mental attribute as a physical one.

In Chapter 3 we discussed the importance of a strong belief system in attaining success in racing. Herb Elliott, the great Australian middle-distance athlete who was unbeaten as a senior over 1500 m and the mile, and who lowered the world 1500 m and mile records in 1958 and 1960, had an exceptionally strong belief system. His golden rule was to train for mental toughness rather than physical development. He believed that if the mind was focused, the physical side would follow.

An increasing number of coaches are recognizing (or at least paying lip service to) the importance of training the mind. Surprisingly, however, it appears that only a minority of runners are taking this dimension of the sport seriously.

The capacity of the mind is one of the great unknown quantities. No-one is certain what it has to offer, how to train it and how, precisely, to harness its strength. While no one, no matter how mentally tough, is ever likely to win a marathon if they have not prepared themselves physically, if equally trained athletes are running together towards the end of a marathon, it is the one who is mentally stronger, or has the better trained mind, who will win. Witness 1994 Comrades victor Alberto Salazar's one metre victory in the 1982 Boston Marathon. His victory over the equally brilliant Dick Beardsley was the result of mental (perhaps even spiritual) and not physical factors.

This century has resulted in substantial improvements in running performances, as vastly improved knowledge about physiological aspects of running is translated into improved training programmes, better diets, and generally healthier lifestyles. We believe that the twenty-first century could lead to further improvements, not as a result of superior physical training methods, but due to a fuller understanding of the resources of our minds.

PRINCIPLE 18:
Use both art and science

Richard Turnbull, who coached Mathews Temane to a world half-marathon best time, believes that good coaching is 40% science and 60% art. In order to run your best, you need to tap into the best of both these worlds.

Without the wisdom of science, which can give vital information concerning factors such as fitness levels, diet and muscle balance, and which can help to prevent overtraining, injury and dehydration, your running career may end in pain and frustration. Without art, however, you will never achieve the finesse derived from those intuitive skills which

Coach Richard Turnbull believes that 60% of coaching is art. The Turnbull-Temane team proved a powerful force in the 1980s, with Mathews Temane using his coach's insights to win countless races, such as this one in Durban in 1988

enable you to tune in to your body's requirements on a level beyond the reach of science. And if you are a coach, the artistic dimension demands that you understand the character, moods and temperament of each of your athletes individually, in order to understand the mental and psychological context within which to best apply scientific principles of training.

Part of the artistic dimension of running relates to Principle 4: your training schedule is always subservient to· what your body tells you. Perhaps the best-known South African example of an athlete who is capable of listening to his body is Bruce Fordyce. Never shy of heavy training, Fordyce has been blessed with the artistry to know when to train hard and when to back off, when to apply effort in a race and when to hold back. Further afield, Sebastian Coe's unerring ability to adjust his training according to his perception of his body's responses to training stress, was a major factor in his athletic successes.

Knowing your own personal bodyprint is essential if you are to run your best

However, we suspect that the majority of athletes and coaches fail to grasp the importance of the artistic side of running your best. Perhaps they are becoming, or producing, '40% only' athletes.

PRINCIPLE 19:
Know your individual training bodyprint

This principle is really the practical expression of the 'art' dimension of Principle 18. Every athlete is different. While the 21 Principles of Running Your Best have general application to all athletes, the specific details will vary from individual to individual. In particular, the relative emphasis that different athletes place on different aspects of their training will vary.

The only way for you to determine what is most appropriate for you, is to carefully observe how you respond to different training methods. You should continue experimenting until you finally discover the training methods that produce the best results for you, regardless of how unusual they may be, or whether or not they work for others.

Essentially, the two critical aspects of training which you must monitor are rest and speed. We are convinced that the secret of reaching the limit of your potential depends on the correct application of these facets, described in some detail in Principles 8 and 9. Too much rest, and you will be deficient in stamina and power; too little, and you are likely to become demotivated, and will be unable to train with sufficient intensity when required. Likewise, too much speed and you run the risk of overtraining, too little and you will find yourself racing on untrained muscle fibres.

There is a school of thought which suggests that the training requirements of running your best are now clearly known and are universal. We do not agree. Clearly, some athletes are physically and mentally less able to adapt to heavier mileages or more speed training than others. Their bodies will break down before they can reap the benefits of this type of training. Some athletes will perform poorly on large doses of relatively slow distance running, while others are able to race well under this type of training.

It is up to you, the unique never-to-be-repeated individual, to discover what works for you in your particular context at work and at home; in other words, what best fits your bodyprint. This leads on to the next principle.

PRINCIPLE 20:
Understand the concept of holism

The concept of holism has a two-fold significance for runners. First of all, it is important that a training programme incorporates sessions which will apply optimal stress to each physiological component that contributes to running success. Training different muscle groups, the cardiovascular system, the metabolism of the entire body, and the mind should all receive specific attention if you are to run your best. An approach to the specificity of training is discussed under Principle 6.

Secondly, holism means that an optimal training programme should recognize the fact that we have responsibilities, pressures and demands on us other than the need or desire to run our best. We live in an era where athletics has become a professional sport in all but name, the International Amateur Athletics Association being one of the most notable anachronisms of our time. Those elite athletes who earn a living from running, must accommodate their

Two married couples who beat the 'running widow or widower' syndrome are Darren and Colleen de Reuck (left) and Grace and Eloi de Oliveira. Darren acts as Colleen's coach, and the de Oliveiras run together. They recently broke the Two Oceans 'husbands and wives' record

non-running activities around their training programmes and racing schedules. For most of us, however, it is the other way around. We must take careful account of our work and home lives and responsibilities before we design our training programme. This way, we can avoid the mistake of allowing our running to become just one more stress in a busy life.

For the majority of runners who have time constraints, we have found that a weekly distance of between 50 and 80 km is optimal for base training. Weekly totals can increase to between 80 km and 120 km for the six to ten week conditioning phase.

Heavy training (either extremely high weekly distances, or a high percentage of quality sessions) unquestionably affects creativity. It also interferes with other commitments, and may introduce adverse stresses such as inadequate sleep, excessive fatigue, family displeasure, and missed deadlines. We suggest in Chapter 7 that running enhances one's productivity and creativity. Here we must admit that too much training can have the opposite effect.

A probable explanation for this is that heavy training causes depletion of certain brain chemicals, the reduction of which also explains the relaxing and tranquillizing effects of running. This relaxing effect is also the reason why serious runners find it difficult to keep down jobs that demand excessive mental effort, particularly in the afternoons, and especially during periods of intensive training.

The converse also appears to be true. Commitment to work which places heavy demands on your creative energy will compromise your ability to follow a training programme which has failed to take account of that commitment.

Another aspect of this Principle is that the athlete needs to avoid falling prey to the Selfish Runner's Syndrome. Even within the context of a book on running your best, we believe that it is vital to reproduce the rules (also listed in *Lore of Running*) which will help you to avoid this syndrome. To put all our reason for living into racing is obviously inappropriate and may ultimately be harmful. Thus we suggest the following guidelines:

- Limit serious running to every second year and then for only a few months of that year.
- Run to and from work if at all possible. Alternatively, run in the early morning, or during your lunch-hour or both.
- Never run after returning home unless you have gone home earlier than normal and have announced your intentions well in advance.
- Do your share of household chores. Most of us dislike housework, but leaving chores undone irritates family and housemates, and provides the runner's spouse with a visible reminder of their status as a running widower or widow.
- Be aware of danger times. The first hour after returning home from work is the time when the needs of the family are at their most demanding; children need their homework, bath-time or bedtime supervised, the evening meal must be prepared, and so forth. This is not the time to leaf through running magazines which have arrived in the day's post, phone up running mates, or worst of all, go out for a run. Weekends must also be handled carefully; your running should conflict as little as possible with the family's weekend recreation.
- Runners with families or partners may have to adapt their plans for peak performance for the sake of their nearest and dearest. Running your best should always be done within the context of your marriage and other important relationships, and not at their expense. Extremely rigorous training should be taken up only for a limited and mutually agreed upon period.
- Never complain about tiredness; don't nag to go home early on evenings out; don't constantly talk about running; and play down the importance of running when in company.

- Be creative. You can pleasurably involve the family in a training session by running alongside your spouse's or children's road or mountain bicycles, or you can take your baby or toddler for an outing in a modified 'running buggy'.
- Where possible, use training to fulfil dual purposes. Commuting, especially, could be turned into a morning or afternoon training session, while errands and visits to friends could also be undertaken on foot, and could add to the logbook. (This would be inappropriate for specific, quality sessions.)

We like the story told by Tom Osler about his friend Ted Corbett, America's first ultra-distance runner. Corbett, who was running an average of 200 km a week at the time, was introduced at a dinner party by his wife as: 'My Ted, who likes to do a little jogging now and then'. On hearing this, Osler nearly choked on his dinner. He could not understand how Corbett had been able to hide the extent of his running from his wife. No doubt he had followed all the guidelines listed above!

PRINCIPLE 21:
Understand the limitations of age and gender

These limitations have been explored in detail in Chapter 1, and we summarize the most important points here.

The important concept to grasp, whether we are older or younger, male or female, gifted or average, is that in striving to run our best we should recognize our physical limitations and set our goals accordingly. Age-specific and gender-group competitions enable us to compete with those whose physical limitations are similar to our own. Figure 1.3 (see p. 26) will assist you if you wish to make equivalent comparisons between your performances and those of runners who are at their peak-performing age.

An important factor in recognizing our physical limitations is that where age is concerned, we need to take account of the number of years in which we have been active as runners in addition to our biological age. It would appear that after fifteen to twenty years of competitive running (possibly only ten if training and racing during these years were at high intensity), performances start to undergo a noticeable decline.

Sonja Laxton wins the 1993 national marathon title at senior level at the age of 45. Her form has remained remarkably consistent throughout her years as a veteran

On the other hand, 40-year-old athletes who have only been competing for a few years are still able to perform strongly. The leading veteran and master runners are almost never those who were elite runners as seniors, but those either relatively new to the sport or those who have made a come-back after a prolonged break from the sport.

Three times world cross-country champion, Portugal's Carlos Lopes, set a world marathon best of 2:07:11 at Rotterdam in 1985 at the age of 38 years (his third cross-country title that year). His feats just short of his fortieth birthday shook the world, but in terms of running years, Lopes was comparatively young, having been sidelined from competition for many years through injury.

On the other hand, Bruce Fordyce has discovered that at 38, he is too 'old' to be a Comrades winner; not because of his chronological age, but because of his years of heavy training and hard racing.

Another 'aging' factor is the number of races run at maximum intensity. We do not believe that this applies to relatively short races (probably up to 20 km), but it is apparent that elite runners are able to run a limited number of marathons at the highest possible intensity, perhaps as few as three. Thereafter, it seems possible that slight but long-term muscle damage prevents these athletes from ever again emulating their earlier performances.

Summary Table of 21 Principles

Principle 1: Constantly re-evaluate your condition, progress and races and set achievable (new) goals

Principle 2: Do the minimum amount of training to achieve your goal

Principle 3: Beware of the Greedy Runner Syndrome

Principle 4: Your training schedule is always subservient to what your body tells you

Principle 5: Vary your training as much as possible

Principle 6: Every session should have a specific function

Principle 7: Plan medium- and long-term programmes which incorporate specific, but non-exclusive, phases

Principle 8: Incorporate recovery periods in regular cycles

Principle 9: Train first for stamina, then for speed

Principle 10: Train at maximum intensity only for limited periods

Principle 11: Don't race when training and race distances in excess of 15 km infrequently

Principle 12: Never train to exhaustion

Principle 13: Incorporate aerobic training to maintain or regain enthusiasm

Principle 14: Understand the principle of peaking

Principle 15: Ensure you undergo an adequate taper prior to racing

Principle 16: Train more than once per day only after careful evaluation

Principle 17: Do not underestimate the importance of mental preparation

Principle 18: Use both art and science

Principle 19: Know your individual training bodyprint

Principle 20: Understand the concept of holism

Principle 21: Understand the limitations of age and gender

TRAINING THE BODY:
Additional training tips

5

TRAINING TIP 1:
Train with a coach

The majority of runners will probably never have the experience of being trained by a coach. Some will have access to training advice from one or more sources, but only a few will enjoy the benefits to be gained from a coach who can give individual attention to runners.

This is unfortunate, as a coach can provide insight into our training weaknesses more easily and objectively than ourselves. Many runners have the ability to prepare themselves physically for a race. However, most of us are less able to provide the motivation and inspiration that a good coach is able to give.

We have seen that coaching involves both art and science (Principle 18). Scientific facts concerning training are readily available. It is the intuitive and 'artistic' skills involved in understanding the forces which motivate individual athletes, as well as the knowledge of how best to harness those forces, which determines greatness in a coach.

In particular, a coach can advise on when we may be straying into 'Greedy Runner Syndrome' territory, and into the realm of overtraining.

TRAINING TIP 2:
Keep a detailed logbook

If you only buy one running-related book (apart from this one!), make it a logbook. A well-kept logbook will become a most valuable possession in your quest to run your best. By comparing present training information with that recorded in past years, you can gain valuable clues as to your current condition, and how to approach your next race.

Essential information that should be recorded in the logbook includes the date, the training route, the details of the training session, what shoes were worn, the running time and distance, running partners and the weather. Additional information can be valuable in assessing whether you are overtraining. This includes the following:

- a note on how each run felt (particularly with respect to muscle soreness);
- the effort rating of each run (perceived intensity);
- the enjoyment rating of each run;
- the waking pulse rate (if it suddenly increases more than five beats a minute above the normal rate, the athlete has done too much the previous day, and should either train very little that day or rest completely);
- the early morning and post-workout body weights;
- the time of going to bed, and the number of hours' sleep;
- the heart rate at the end of each interval during speed training. (Those with heart rate monitors can keep more detailed records of resting and exercising heart rates);
- women should record their menstrual cycles so that they can check whether this influences their performance.

TRAINING TIP 3:
Learn how to breathe properly

Yoga-breathing or 'belly-breathing' is the correct way to breathe. This involves breathing predominantly with the diaphragm, rather than with the chest muscles. With belly-breathing, the chest hardly moves at all, while the stomach rises as you breathe in and retracts when you exhale.

Belly-breathing prevents the development of the 'stitch'. The anatomical reasons for this are discussed in *Running Injuries* and *Lore of Running*. Other ways to prevent the 'stitch' occurring are by avoiding food and water for two to four hours before exercise, and by training the abdominal muscles with appropriate sit-ups.

TRAINING TIP 4:
Train with company

Although distance running is often associated with solitude (one thinks of the loneliness of the long-distance runner), it is best to run with others, especially when starting training. This helps to maintain interest and motivation, and makes training an enjoyable social occasion.

Runners and cars don't mix well. Here Tim Stewart gives a vehicle a wide berth

However, sociability is only one aspect, and there can be dangers in group running. These relate to the fact that the pace of the group may not be appropriate for you. By running too slowly you may feel frustrated, and may not stress your muscle fibres sufficiently. By running too far and fast, you may not incorporate sufficient recovery sessions and may reach an overtrained state, in which you are prone to illness and injury.

For this reason, women should be wary of training with men on a regular basis. Darren de Reuck, husband and coach of top South African distance athlete, Colleen de Reuck, admitted that Colleen had been racing sub-optimally for some time before they realized that this was because she trained daily with a group of elite male athletes, and never trained at 'recovery' pace.

TRAINING TIP 5:
At first, train only on the flat

Untrained persons would be well advised to run on hills only when you can comfortably run on the flat for 30 minutes. Once this has been achieved, hill-training can play an essential role in preparing yourself to run your best.

TRAINING TIP 6:
Run in scenic areas

In order to maintain enthusiasm, you should vary your routes as much as possible (Principle 5), and try to run in scenic surroundings. This will stimulate you mentally, and enable you to take on increased training loads while enjoying the trip. In particular, your routes on long runs should be chosen on this basis, and should be off main roads as far as possible.

TRAINING TIP 7:
When on the road, run defensively

Although we advocate training off major road routes where possible, it is inevitable that much, if not most of our training will take place in the company of motor cars. Take care to observe standard safety rules of the road, and run defensively. Don't add to the growing number of runners who have been seriously injured or killed while training.

TRAINING TIP 8:
Do regular stretching and strengthening exercises

This relates to Principle 20 (understand the holism of training.) Because running is not a symmetrical activity, it leads to muscle imbalances, mainly the strengthening of the muscles on the backs of the legs (calves and hamstrings), as well as the gluteal and back muscles, at the expense of weak abdominal muscles. This frequently leads to lower back pain due to pressure on the spine.

This imbalance should be corrected in two ways: by strengthening the abdominal muscles, and stretching the back muscles. We have provided a series of exercises for his athletes aimed at strengthening the abdominal muscles without straining the back. These can be found in Appendix 2, pp. 232-7.

Stretching exercises should also be done regularly, preferably before and after each run. A stretch should be held for at least 10 seconds to be effective, and the 'bobbing' method (bouncing up and down) should never be used.

Stretching is a vital part of a safe training programme. Lindsay Weight demonstrates

Three to five sets for each relevant muscle group should be undertaken. *Running Injuries* and *Lore of Running* describe a full set of stretching exercises, and we include the most important of these in Appendix 2, pp. 228-30.

TRAINING TIP 9:
Eat as you feel you need to

The special nutritional requirements of endurance athletes are described in detail in Chapter 8. All the beginner needs to know is that his or her body will, by and large, dictate its requirements. There is thus no need to follow a special diet. However, it is generally helpful for runners to reduce the amount of fat and increase the carbohydrates in their diet.

TRAINING TIP 10:
Ensure that you get sufficient sleep

Although the amount of time that individuals sleep can vary quite remarkably, with some sleeping as little as four hours a night, the average person sleeps between seven and eight hours a night. With harder training, the amount of time one needs to sleep definitely increases. If you are in high intensity training, you are likely to need at least nine hours of sleep per night.

TRAINING TIP 11:
Take weather conditions into account

Special precautions need to be taken if one wishes to exercise in severe environmental conditions. For milder weather conditions, we would advise the following precautions:

- Firstly, don't exercise vigorously in the very early morning if the temperature is very cold (below freezing). It seems that the likelihood of developing upper respiratory tract infections is increased if one consistently trains very hard in very cold air.
- Secondly, wear a 'rain suit' if it is raining heavily and there is a strong wind blowing. Wind increases the wind-chill factor, and could cause the runner whose clothes are wet to develop a critical reduction in body temperature (hypothermia). See Chapter 2 for more details.

TRAINING THE BODY:
Women and children

6

TRAINING AND WOMEN RUNNERS

Menstruation and osteoporosis

Some years ago, it was noticed that competitive female track and distance runners had a high incidence of irregular menstrual periods. In fact, 50% of a group of competitive 10 km runners who trained more than 80 km per week, had fewer than three periods per year, a condition known as amenorrhoea. At the time it was believed that firstly, the disturbed menstruation was a direct result of the exercise and specifically the running, as women swimmers and cyclists who trained even harder than these runners did not have such a high incidence of menstrual irregularity. Secondly, it was thought that the absence of menstruation was probably beneficial, as this meant that the training of the women concerned was not interrupted by their periods. We now know that both these ideas are incorrect.

First of all, exercise alone does not cause any major or sustained changes in menstrual patterns. Rather it appears that running, and especially competitive distance running, attracts women at risk of developing menstrual irregularity. Such women are thin, psychologically-driven and highly competitive individuals, who have usually had a history of menstrual irregularity before starting running. Most importantly, runners at risk of menstrual cessation often eat poorly in order to maintain low levels of body fat. In fact, there is a strong correlation between abnormal eating behaviours, including bingeing and vomiting (bulimia nervosa) and anorexia nervosa, and disturbed menstrual patterns. Thus, we now teach that one must assume that a female distance runner with amenorrhoea or other menstrual disturbances has an eating disorder until this possibility is excluded.

Secondly, there is now a large body of evidence showing that even minor changes in menstrual patterns are deleterious, as they cause a loss of minerals from the bones, a condition known as osteoporosis. This is because the female hormone oestrogen is the most powerful determinant of bone mineral density in women; therefore, any sustained reduction in the circulating oestrogen concentrations (as occurs when there is any disturbance in menstrual patterns), will cause a progressive loss of bone minerals. It has been shown, for example, that if a woman of 25 loses her menstrual periods for two to three years, she will be left with a bone mineral density similar to that of a 55-year-old woman.

This early development of osteoporosis in young female runners who experience menstrual irregularities also increases their risk of developing stress fractures, as described in *Running Injuries*. As a result of these findings, we now describe a triad of features that may be present in some female distance runners. This triad is made up of menstrual irregularity, osteoporosis with or without stress fractures, and an eating disorder. Hence when any one of these features is present, it is important to determine whether or not the other two are also present.

The practical implications are that young female runners who have menstrual irregularities should be informed of the deleterious long-term effects that this condition will have on their bones, and the need to resume normal menstrual periods as a matter of priority. Many will understand the need for treatment more easily if they have already suffered a stress fracture that has interfered with their running.

When the cause of the menstrual abnormality is an eating disorder that is resistant to correction, it is then advised that the runner receive replacement oestrogen therapy in the form of the Pill. This should be prescribed in consultation with the runner's gynaecologist.

The good news is that if menstrual irregularity is treated early, the amount of bone mineral loss will be curtailed, and the continual increase in bone mineral content that occurs in normally-menstruating women up to the age of 32 to 35 years will resume. As a result, the woman's bone mineral content will increase and her bone age will once more approach that of a younger person. However, the duration of the untreated menstrual irregularity will determine to what degree the optimal bone mineral density (reached between the age of 32 and 35) is achieved; the shorter the duration of menstrual irregularity, the closer to normal the peak bone density.

Training and pregnancy

What of the woman runner who is pregnant? There are two extreme views regarding exercise during pregnancy. The one, similar to that prescribed for all pregnant women at the turn of the century, is that no exercise whatsoever should be undertaken. The other is that the pregnant runner need make no alteration in her exercise programme.

The truth, as usual, lies somewhere in between. There is good evidence to suggest that maintaining an appropriate level of physical fitness during pregnancy is beneficial for the expectant mother, and aids delivery without jeopardizing the health of the foetus in any way. An appropriate level of physical training might be, for example, as much as 30–60 minutes a day of moderate exercise, the intensity of which is gradually reduced as the added weight of the baby makes weight-bearing exercise (such as running) progressively more difficult. If the habitual level of exercise is less than this amount, there is no need to increase it. The point is that while moderate amounts of exercise are beneficial during pregnancy, this is not the time to start a more intensive training programme.

Five of South Africa's best women runners after taking the first five places in a 5 km road race: from left, Terri-Lee Bedford, Marietjie McDermott, Elana Meyer, Nicole Whiteford and Sonja Laxton

Women who compete in distance events pose a more difficult problem, especially if they race frequently as professionals. Our concern is that their intensive training and racing
programmes will cause their body temperatures to be elevated for prolonged periods on a daily basis, and especially
on the occasions that they compete in 15–42 km races. It is
known that sustained elevations in body temperature (such
as occur in maternal viral infections) may cause foetal
abnormalities, especially if they occur in the first three
months of pregnancy. Accordingly, we advise runners to
stop competitive training and racing as soon as they fall
pregnant, and to revert to a more moderate training programme. It is probable that this approach is too conservative, and that the risk in continuing heavy training is probably
overstated. However, in the absence of definitive evidence
proving that competitive racing and training is safe during
pregnancy, it would seem that the soundest approach is to
practice caution in the interests of the unborn child.

TRAINING AND CHILDREN: special concerns

'The problem of a young athlete giving up is not usually the
child's doing,' says Zola Budd-Pieterse, who was herself a
child athletics wonder. 'The biggest problem is pushy
parents.' Zola saw scores of promising young athletes 'burn
out' around her, while she was competing in her high school
years. The reason she was different (she still competes successfully at the highest level) was that she was never pushed.
In fact, her parents and teachers had to hold her back!

While there is evidence to suggest that intensive training
at a relatively early age may be necessary in order to
become a world-class swimmer, gymnast, cricketer or tennis
player, this is certainly not the case with respect to
endurance sports, notably athletics. It is the exception rather
than the rule for children who have excelled in athletics to
go on to triumph at senior level. Furthermore, there is evidence to suggest that intensive training during childhood
does not appear to have any particular benefits that could
not be achieved by similar training after the age of 18 years.

*Zola Budd was winning races by the time she was 14. Always self-
motivated, her parents and coaches had to hold her back, rather
than push her – possibly the key to her enduring success as an
athlete*

Fifteen years after her initial successes, Zola Budd-Pieterse is still winning races. Former 800 m athlete Van Zyl Naude's support as a coach and friend has been an important factor

The South African experience

South Africa has produced junior athletes of exceptional ability, but these athletes have largely failed to sustain this standard at senior level. For example, a squad of 12 South African athletes was sent to the World Junior Championships at Seoul in 1992, with just a few weeks' notice. Ten of the athletes qualified for the finals, with three winning medals (one silver and two bronze). At the 1994 Junior Championships in Lisbon, young South African athletes did even better, winning three gold medals. In contrast, only three senior-level athletes out of a team of 20 qualified for the finals at the 1993 World Championships in Stuttgart (excluding two in the marathon, which was an automatic final), with not a single athlete winning a medal.

Limited competitive years

We saw in Principle 21 that it is probable that runners have limited time as competitive athletes. This could be as little as ten years, if training is done at high intensity during this period. In other words, if you began hard training at the age of 12, you might find yourself approaching the twilight of

Meck Mothuli, winner of the world half-marathon junior title in 1993 at the age of 17

your career at 22, probably while still short of your physical and mental peak.

Many of the world's top coaches discourage intense training for athletes who are younger than 18 years old. 'Do what you enjoy and don't get too serious about it,' is Herb Elliott's advice to these athletes, an attitude which appears to be winning universal support. Running guru Doctor George Sheehan was also a fervent advocate of children experiencing the fun rather than the competitiveness of the sport, even though he recognized that children do have physiological advantages: 'Kilogram for kilogram, the nine-year-old is the world's best endurance athlete. And he moves with the grace and elegance of the free animal. He has ... the biggest heart volume for his weight that he will ever have unless he is an Olympic champion. He is the nearest thing to perpetual motion in human form that you will ever see.'

How much and how far?

Given that many children will want to run and race within the limits of enjoyment of the sport, how much should they train and how far should they race?

Grete Waitz, arguably the greatest female distance athlete the world has seen, advises that specialization in middle-distance races (800 m to 1 500 m) should not take place before the runner is 13 to 14 years old. She goes on to advocate that races of up to 10 km should not be tackled in earnest before the age of 15 or 16. Prior to specializing, runners should take part in a balanced training programme, which should emphasise easy aerobic conditioning.

To assist younger runners, we offer the following guidelines. While they may err on the conservative side, we believe that if they are followed, they will allow athletes to develop their full potential. Because children mature at different rates, our guidelines should be interpreted in the light of their particular development framework.

- 6 to 10 years: the emphasis should be on the fun of exercise and sports in general. Running should mostly be related to games and should not be an end in itself. Racing should be limited to schools' sports days and fun events. Training regimes will have little effect, as children lack the hormones to adapt to training.
- 11 to 14 years: at this age, children can begin to learn proper techniques and principles of running, as they are now able to begin to adapt to training. In general, training loads should be no more than one-third of what an adult could tolerate. The emphasis should be on short bursts of sprinting, and longer recovery jogs.

  15 to 18 years: teenagers can adapt to training loads of about one-half to two-thirds of those of an adult. These children are mentally and physically ready for more specialised training and relatively intensive competition, although the ability of individuals to cope with the mental and physical demands of this competition will vary. Some will be content to train for a few weeks a year for school sports, while others, such as Zola Budd-Pieterse (who broke the world 5 000 m record at the age of 17), and Potchefstroom schoolboy, Hezekiel Sepeng (who ran fifth in the 800 m at the 1993 senior-level World Championships at 18 and second in the 1996 Olympic 800 m at 21), will seek higher honours.

South African Road Running has recognised the wisdom of encouraging younger runners to focus on shorter distance events, by placing age restrictions on road races as follows:

Hezekiel Sepeng, 800 m silver medallist at the 1994 Commonwealth Games at the age of 19 and Olympic 800 m silver medallist at 21

Age (years)	Maximum Distance Race
8 - 11	5 km
12 - 13	10 km
14 - 15	15 km
16 - 17	32 km
18	no restriction

Burning carbos or burning out?

Two issues often raised about children involved in endurance exercise, such as swimming or running, are the question of diet and whether the child is likely to suffer burnout symptoms. With respect to diet, there is no evidence to suggest that children engaged in strenuous exercise require special diets which differ from those of adults. Hence the principles discussed in Chapter 8 apply equally for children. Unless children are racing or training over excessive distances (and we strongly urge that they should not do so), a normal, well-balanced diet should be sufficient. If the child on a normal diet reaches the stage where supplements are required as a result of strenuous exercise, we would suggest that the level of exercise may be inappropriate.

Young runners such as these should be encouraged to run for the pleasure of the sport

Equally, there is no evidence to suggest that children are more prone to physical burnout than adults. While overtraining can easily occur, this can be overcome by resting for up to six weeks. What is perhaps more of a threat to children involved in competitive endurance sport, is mental burnout as a result of continuously following tough and monotonous training regimes, for which neither their minds nor their bodies are adapted.

Heat and (stunted) growth

Further issues which must be considered are the ability of children to adapt to exercise in heat, and the question of whether endurance exercise is likely to stunt the child's growth. Children who run are not able to adapt as well as their adult counterparts to exercising in heat. They produce proportionately more body heat during exercise, have a lower sweating capacity and ability to transfer heat in the body than adults, are more likely to absorb heat from the atmosphere, and acclimatise to heat less rapidly than adults.

Children should thus limit exercising in hot conditions to 30 minutes at the most, and should allow a two-week adaption programme when moving to a hotter climate. They should wear light and porous clothing to facilitate body heat loss, and should drink fluids at regular intervals during exercise.

Although the cartilaginous growth plate which separates the bone shaft from its ends in children only solidifies into bone between the ages of 15 and 19, there is little evidence to suggest running could be the cause of stunted growth. (The predominance of short, slightly-built athletes in distance running relates to the physical advantages enjoyed by these athletes, rather than to any growth inhibition caused by running!) There is, however, a slight risk of damage to the growth plate through injury incurred by participating in a contact sport. This could lead to unequal limb growth.

Fragile egos

A major problem for potential world-class athletes is that they often have to satisfy the fragile egos of manipulative parents and teachers/coaches. In these cases, the adults are often those who have failed to achieve, and who push their children or pupils to the limit in order to bask in their reflected glory. Child athletes in this position have little chance to achieve greatness beyond junior status.

Hopefully, an increasing number of parents and teachers will learn to follow the advice of the great New Zealand coach, Arthur Lydiard: 'Encourage young athletes, but don't force them; let them play at athletics...'

7 TRAINING THE MIND

In 1991, the Natal rugby team defeated Northern Transvaal, South Africa's traditional rugby giants, by a large margin in an interprovincial encounter. Some weeks later, the two teams met again, and this time the result was reversed, with an even greater margin of victory. Assuming honest endeavour on the part of the teams in both encounters, what was the mystery factor which resulted in so complete a turnabout in the fortunes of the two sides? Given the relatively short time between the matches, this reversal of fortunes could not have been related to playing skills or even physical preparation for the matches, which must have been reasonably constant.

Could psychological factors have been the key? The Northern Transvaal team, which had gone into the first match in a state of complacency, were keenly motivated by the desire to put the earlier humiliation behind them second time around, and their effectiveness on the sporting field was transformed as a result.

Another fine example of the importance of mental fortitude can be seen in the performance of the cricketer Jonty Rhodes. He invariably performs best when the mental demands on him are greatest, and his team has its back to the wall. Witness his unbeaten century on the last day of the first test against Sri Lanka in 1993, an innings which saved South Africa from defeat. One also thinks of his 76 not out in the second innings of the 1994 Sydney test against Australia, which set up one of the most improbable cricketing victories of all time. At school, Rhodes' cricket coach had a favourite line: whenever his team was in a completely hopeless position, he would remark: `Ah, but it's good to be alive'.

Then there is the golfer Seve Ballesteros, who was asked in his youth what his thoughts would be if he had to play a ten metre putt to win his first major golfing tournament, which, if missed, would lose him the tournament. His answer was that he had dreamed of and worked towards being in exactly such a position all his life.

Five decades ago the great running analyst, Arthur Newton, wrote: 'Stamina seems to me to be just as much a mental attribute as a physical one.' It has been shown that not only stamina, but the ability to achieve top performances, is strongly influenced by one's mental fortitude. Yet fifty years after Newton penned these words, this is still the most neglected aspect in the training programmes of most athletes. Some athletes pay lip service to the role of the mind in achieving sporting success; we often hear the saying, 'the Comrades Marathon is 90% mental, and only 10% physical effort'. Their training programmes, however, scarcely reflect this balance. Possibly less than 1% of their preparation time for the race is devoted to mental preparation.

Is this because of a belief that mental toughness is purely genetically determined – either you have it or you don't? Or is it because of a lack of understanding of how to train the mind? This leads to further questions: what role does the mind indeed play in running performance? How can we begin to unlock the hidden resources of the mind? Are there psychological benefits to embrace, or dangers to avoid as we continue in our chosen sport? We will attempt to explore these questions more fully in this chapter.

THE POWER OF THE MIND IN SPORT

The brick wall

Almost 40 years after the four-minute-mile barrier was broken for the first time, the 'dream mile' remains one of the most sought-after targets for middle-distance athletes. The struggle to break through that barrier for the first time, and subsequent efforts to run below 3:50 for the distance provide a vivid illustration of the role of the mind in athletics.

Figure 7.1 plots the progress of the mile record since 1913. What interests us, in the context of the power of the mind in sport, is the fact that the two longest bottlenecks in the progression of the mile through history have occurred immediately prior to decisive mental barriers – four minutes and 3:50. A similar bottleneck can be noted prior to the breaking of the 4:10 barrier, but the relative lack of competition at this time renders any conclusion as to the cause of this particular delay suspect.

No doubt there are a variety of reasons for these chronological bottlenecks, but there is equally little doubt that one

Jonty Rhodes: his mental fortitude has helped to elevate him to world class standards on the cricket field

The Argus

of the primary causes, and probably the major cause, was that the minds of the leading mile athletes of the time prevented them from running at the speeds of which they were physically capable.

Finally, when those barriers were broken, it was the athletes with the toughest minds (Roger Bannister, 3:59,4 in 1954 and John Walker, 3:49,4 in 1975) who were successful. Bannister, who more than anyone else at the time perceived that the battle for the sub-4 minute mile was fought in the mind, not the body, was well aware of the importance of psychological preparation. He conditioned his mind so that it would 'release in four short minutes the energy I usually spend in half an hour's training.'

Revealingly, it was the top Australian miler of the fifties, John Landy, whom many considered more physiologically gifted than Bannister, and who had run the mile faster than 4:03 on six occasions by April 1954, who said: 'It is a brick wall. I shall not attempt it again.' Weeks later on May 6, 1954, Bannister carved out his niche in history, running a 58,9 second final lap in a superbly planned race at the Iffley Road track at Oxford, and recording 3:59,4 for the four-lap event.

Figure 7.1
Evolution of world mile record

This shows the progress of the world mile record and illustrates the role of the mind in striving to run our best. Note that the longest bottlenecks occur immediately prior to a significant 'time marker'. These become mental rather than physiological barriers for those attempting the improve on the record. Other bottlenecks were an eight year span prior to Jules Ladounegue breaking the 4:10 barrier in 1931, a similar period before John Walker bettered the 3:50 mile, and a third prior to Noureddine Morceli running inside the 3:45 mark. How long before the mile is run under 3:40?

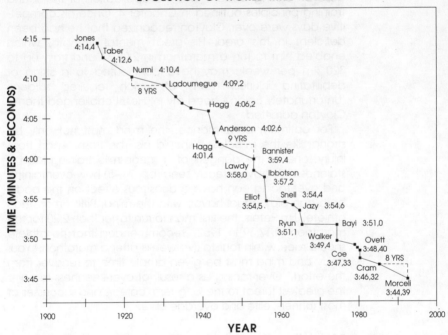

EVOLUTION OF WORLD MILE RECORD

Just six weeks after Bannister's success, possibly after realizing that the 'brick wall' was in his mind, Landy ran the mile in 3:58,0. Whether he would have achieved this had Bannister not succeeded in piloting the way through the 'wall' at Oxford, will never be known. We suspect that he would not have done so.

Mental strength and running wisdom

Derek Clayton, who held the world marathon record (2:08:33) for 12 years, believed that mental fortitude was the key to his success: 'I ran believing in mind over matter'. Like Bannister before him, Clayton was completely focused on his goal, and when his physical resources were depleted, his mental tenacity often enabled him to achieve his target, most notably when he became the first marathoner to run faster than 2:10 for the standard distance.

We should note, however, that mental strength can be a two-edged sword, and needs to be combined with a good dose of running wisdom and the application of the sound training principles outlined in Chapter 4. Once his competitive days were over, Clayton recognized that he had been deficient in this area. His great mental strength, which enabled him to run a marathon in 2:08:33 and train up to 320 km per week, may have contributed to a string of debilitating injuries, many of which required surgery. 'Unfortunately I didn't heed my injuries, I challenged them,' Clayton admitted.

For optimum performance, the mind must not only be strong; like the muscles, it should also be fresh. Apart from injury, one of the dangers of a mega-mile training load is staleness. We have already seen (pp. 71–5) how overtraining and over-racing can have a disastrous effect on the body; both can play equal havoc with the mind. British marathon athlete, Jim Peters, the first man to run faster than 2:20 for the marathon (2:17:39 in 1952), recommended that no athlete should race within four to five weeks after a marathon: 'Your body and mind must be given ample time to recover from the effort.' Over-racing as a result of over-keenness remains the greatest threat to the long-term careers and successes of most runners, elite and average alike.

Moulding the mind

We will look later at how, just as running training prepares the body for physical exertion, the mind can be similarly prepared to cope with the mental stress that accompanies that exertion. What is important to note here, is that confidence, moulded from a positive belief system and motivation, is a vital aspect of mental strength, which can be honed to take the athlete to the limits posed by his or her physiology. This applies not only to the elite athlete, but to any runner who

Blanche Moila (in front), a pioneer athlete with formidable mental powers, earned national colours at a time when social taboos made running a no-go area for black women

wishes to respond positively, and thus successfully, to racing challenges.

We have often observed how a race leader, on being overtaken, is transformed from a confident, fluid-striding athlete to a demotivated individual running at reduced pace. Once the new leader has opened a clear gap, the pace of the former leader often slows dramatically to leave the unfortunate athlete finishing well down the field, or even dropping out of the race. A similar scenario might occur when an athlete drops off the pace of a 'bus' or group of athletes running together. Once this happens, the runner will often drop back far more rapidly than can be explained by either fatigue or the increased wind resistance which comes into play.

*Mind games:
how do you
respond on
being
overtaken?*

When this happens early in a race, it is quite possibly the
result of over-eagerness on the part of the runner, or a desire
to lead the race for as far as possible (and possibly win television exposure; hence the name 'television runners'). However, when either of these scenarios take place in the latter
stages of a race, the inability of the runner to maintain the
pace, either of the group or of the overtaking runner, is more
likely to be mental than physiological. It is possible that these
runners have been unable to harness the full resources of
the mind, and are thus unable to respond to the challenge
in a positive way. While they may have been physically prepared for the race, they remain mentally under-trained.

At critical stages of a race, it is the mind, more than anything else, which will determine the outcome of the challenge. Whether we have to hold off a strong challenge to
win, or are overtaken by a keen rival, or have to run the final
2 km in just 12 minutes to make the 4 hour 30 minute

marathon cut-off time, our mind will be the key factor in dealing with the situation. If we can prepare our minds to cope with these crises, our performances, and thus the pleasure we derive from the sport, will be enhanced.

PSYCHOLOGICAL PREPARATION

We saw in Chapter 3 that our belief system will determine how we will respond to a race challenge or stimulus. We need to explore here how our belief system is formed, and how it can be modified to produce optimum performance. We will also discuss certain techniques which can enable us to be in control of our thoughts and emotions (which form the way we feel about ourselves, and thus determine our belief system to a large extent). Various aspects of mental preparation for racing are covered in Chapter 9.

Self-concept

We have noted the importance of a positive belief system for optimum competitive performance. Here we explore how we can change ours for the better. In short, how do we set about training our minds?

The difference between a strong or weak belief system is determined primarily by our self-concept (what we believe about ourselves). A multitude of past thoughts, emotions and attitudes form our self-concept, and significant patterns are established by our past performances, our body image (what we honestly believe we can achieve in sport), and the attitude that significant people in our lives, such as our parents, spouse, close friends or coaches, have towards us and our participation in sport. Self-concept is also influenced by what we really think about ourselves (our real self), what we aspire to be (our ideal self), and the difference between the two.

We saw above what happened to the runner who, when leading a race, was caught or overtaken by another athlete. Let's put ourselves in the shoes of that runner. How would we respond in that situation? Would we immediately surge away, would we throw in the towel and drop behind, or would we run with our opponent and plan to break away at a later stage?

Our response would be largely determined by how we process the stimulus of being passed, how we relate it to our

The loneliness of the long-distance runner: Josiah Thungwane on his way to winning the 1993 SA marathon championship race

self-concept, and which thoughts and emotions, particularly those which respond to the possibility of defeat, are aroused. These psychological responses are modified by our attitude to the specific event in which we are competing (i.e. how important it is to us) and, most important, our attitude to the person who is passing us. The following questions might be helpful in determining our attitude: does this athlete's record intimidate me? Do I have a good record against him or her? Do I dislike him or her?

So we begin to comprehend a cyclical chain of events, with each link in the chain (our responses) determining future ones. This feedback system of shaping our self-concept and belief system, and determining our behaviour, is illustrated on p. 136.

The stimulus (in the above scenario, being caught by the runner) activates emotions and thoughts, termed 'self-talk', which will be either positive or negative, thus having either a beneficial or a detrimental effect on your performance. The behaviour that results, whether positive or negative, will feed back into your belief system, reinforcing the chain, so that the next time you are in the same situation, you are more likely to respond in the same way.

An example: in the 1992 Comrades Marathon, Charl Mattheus, who was running in the lead with Mark Page and Nick Bester at 60 km, went through a terrible stage between 65 km and 75 km, to the extent that it looked doubtful whether he would secure a top ten finish. The physical battle he faced was real enough, but he had to engage equally in a mental struggle. As he had trained for a win, he might have gained little satisfaction from a relatively poor position, and the unwelcome stimulus of a body which would not respond, might have tempted a weak response, such as dropping out of the race at that stage. To his credit, Mattheus' mind was equal to the challenge, and he kept running, later to emerge from the trough and power home to a superb victory.

Undoubtedly, Mattheus' belief system would have been immeasurably strengthened through the experience, and he is likely be a tougher competitor in the future as a result. Had he dropped out, his belief system would have been imprinted with the image of a loser; in all probability, when a similar challenge next presented itself, he would have acted as a loser all over again. Contrasting examples of athletes who always fall apart when the pressure is on, particularly during the last 30 km of the Comrades Marathon, are equally obvious.

'Chain' may be an apt metaphor to describe the circle of stimuli and response, as in many senses we are prisoners of our past behaviour patterns, often learnt from our parents who in turn learned those behaviours from their parents. The danger of a negative response (such as fading or dropping out of a race) to a stimulus such as the pain of muscle soreness, or being caught by a runner towards the end of a race, is that the negative response influences our belief system, making it probable that a similar stimulus in a future race will once again invoke the same response.

We have implied that a positive self-concept is associated with a strong belief system. This suggests that the way to modify our belief system – to break the chain of negative responses – is to strengthen our self-concept. Ideally, when we wrestle with the complexities of the thoughts and emotions of the mind, professional help should be sought. Nevertheless, there are several simple techniques that can be used to 'train the mind' to cope more positively with challenging stimuli which may confront us in competitive situations. These are aimed at strengthening the self-concept.

Technique 1: Analysis of past response

By examining our responses to a variety of competitive challenges, we will get a clear idea of the strength of our belief system. When our psychological weaknesses confront us unmistakably in black and white, we may be able to respond more positively when next faced with a challenge which has troubled us in the past.

This points to the need to record accurate, detailed information in our training log books (see pp. 109–10), describing not only our physical condition, but also our mental responses. A practical way of doing this would be to allocate log book space for each race, and to list our responses, in terms of thoughts, emotions and behaviour, to various sporting challenges. This could be done in columns like these:

Stimulus   **Self-talk/belief system**   **Response**
(Thoughts)   *(Emotions and Behaviour)*

We suggest that you first record your response to the challenge in terms of your emotions and behaviour. For example, in the situation we have already imagined – the case of being overtaken by another athlete towards the end of an important race – the emotions that might have been aroused could include fear, anger and frustration at being passed, or, alternatively, joy that another runner was going to make you earn your victory.

The next step is to record the stimulus that caused your particular response, in this case, being passed at a late stage in the race, possibly by a particularly close rival. This could apply equally to situations at the front or nearer the back of the field: we are aware that some of the most competitive race encounters take place among friends and rivals in the slower quarter of the field!

Finally, the thoughts that were evoked by that sporting situation should be listed. In the example that we have given, the thoughts could indicate the belief system of a winner: 'I can stay with her. I'm just as good as she is' – or that of an also-ran: 'I've blown it. I'm a real loser.'

A record of your responses to some 20 to 30 racing situations should lead to a clearer understanding of your belief system, and this will facilitate the strengthening of your self-concept. The analysis will also reveal a clear relationship between a positive belief system and a favourable (winning) response, and will also show the converse – that negative thoughts usually lead to an unfavourable result.

The power of absolute concentration shows on the face of Colleen de Reuck

Technique 2: Reinforcement

The analysis of racing situations outlined above will enable you to become more sensitive to your thought patterns. This will help you to dispute bad or negative thoughts as they occur. In addition, you should practise applying positive self-statements as often as possible in all sporting situations. The more frequently these statements are made, the more likely they are to become fixed beliefs.

A good way to practice disputing negative and reinforcing positive statements, especially once a relatively weak belief system has been unmasked, is to do so in races which you have planned to run at less than maximum effort. You will then be better equipped, physically, to make a positive response when challenged, and although the response will be made under 'artificial' circumstances, it will begin to reinforce a pattern of responses that you will finally be able draw on under true race conditions.

Another way of practising this positive reinforcement technique is to train on the race course, particularly over difficult sections. The stimulus of racing up a steep uphill section late in a race could elicit a weak response – that of walking – under race conditions. Tackling the problematic section under more favourable circumstances in training could help to promote a positive attitude come race day. The climb to Constantia Nek occurs between the 38 and 45 km markers in the 56 km Two Oceans Marathon, and has reduced even the elite to walking pace. Polly Shorts, the steep rise which occurs 78 km into the 'up' Comrades Marathon from Durban to Pietermaritzburg, has much the same effect. If at all possible, these potential nemeses should be run frequently in training, preferably towards the end of long training runs, in order to fashion a positive emotional and behavioural response to that particular stimulus.

Technique 3: Appropriate goal setting

There is nothing quite so damaging to the self-concept as the failure to live up to our own expectations. For this reason, the word 'must' should never be used unless you are one hundred percent certain of achieving an easy goal. If this statement is followed by failure, you will find it very difficult to trust your future beliefs. Failure after a statement such as 'I must win the Olympic Marathon' will have very serious consequences for your belief system, as the unspoken message to yourself is that failure to reach this goal would be a mark of your personal inadequacy. This will undermine whatever confidence you might previously have had in yourself, and will therefore make it even less likely that you will succeed in your next attempt at that goal.

To 'aim high' may appear to be a noble ideal, and the route to success, but in psychological terms it is a dangerous strategy. If we are in a position to plan for the medium- to long-term in our racing career, it would be far better to adopt a conservative approach in setting our goals. Go with targets, at least initially, that are readily achievable. In achieving them you will be strengthening your self-concept and building for future success.

In this respect, Elana Meyer is an ideal example. She says that one of the main reasons for her success in recent years is the fact that she has always set realistic goals, however conservative they may have appeared to be. Each year, for the past ten years, she has been able to improve her time over some distance on the road or track, and this steady progress has kept her motivated to seek further improvements.

A parallel strategy is to set many targets as stepping stones to a major goal, particularly within a single race. This

Much of Elana Meyer's success can be attributed to realistic goal-setting

will be discussed further in Chapter 9. An outline of a goal-setting framework is included for your convenience at the back of this book (see Appendix 3).

Technique 4: The 'schizophrenic' approach
In this technique we put our 'alter egos' to work by letting them cope positively with challenging stimuli, and then trying to let our real selves catch up.

First of all, write down a description of the person you aspire to be – your ideal self. Next, describe the person you actually consider yourself to be, your real person. In these descriptions, include real versus ideal lists of personal attributes, sporting achievements and motivations, dedication and training habits, relationship with coach and team members (if applicable), overall and specific fitness levels, sporting skills or talents, and sporting achievements.

Next, imagine your real and ideal selves are two separate identities following each other around in your daily life. Pay special attention to those attributes of the ideal and real selves that differ the most. The next step is to imagine the two selves in the various sporting situations in which you participate. At first, the ideal self goes through the same

Alberto Salazar has overcome the ten-year hiatus in his career to return as a world champion marathon runner

Touchline Media

motions as the real self; however, the abilities of the ideal self ultimately surpass those of the real self, and so produce the performance you desire.

Now begin to visualize yourself as your ideal self in every-day situations. Finally, imagine how your ideal self would have coped with previous competitive failures. In a similar way, rehearse forthcoming competitive events by imagining how your ideal self would successfully complete such events.

Clearly, these are difficult techniques which are not mastered overnight. Nor are they probably ever developed to maximum benefit without the assistance and advice of a qualified professional, such as a sports psychologist.

Technique 5: Assessing mental cause of failure

We all know of athletes who perform exceptionally in training, only to fail miserably in competition. As medals are not usually handed out for success achieved in training, it may be beneficial to analyze some of the possible reasons for competitive failure. While some such individuals simply over-train, as we saw in the last chapter, it is likely that many others suffer from various psychological syndromes.

One such syndrome is simply the inability to achieve an 'optimum level of arousal' before competition, usually resulting in the excessive expenditure of nervous energy. This is discussed in more detail in Chapter 9. Another syndrome has its roots in the fear of success, which is linked to one or more of the stresses that success can breed. These specific stresses need to be more closely scrutinised. If we can recognise the various root causes of fear of success and modify them, this will lead to a strengthening of the self-concept.

- *Social and emotional isolation*
Success may isolate athletes from their friends and families, in particular their spouses, and may invoke jealousy among others with whom they come into contact. Paradoxically, increased admiration and affirmation by fans only intensifies this loneliness, as fans expect athletes to be superhuman.

- *Guilt about displaying aggression*
Athletes who have been taught since childhood that aggression is 'bad' may have difficulty expressing the necessary aggression during competition. This might be particularly problematic for female athletes, given that the usual socialization that girls experience as children prohibits aggressive and competitive behaviour.

- *Fear of discovering physical limits*
Athletes who as children were rewarded only for winning or for extreme excellence, may be unwilling to test themselves to the limit in case they fail. They therefore rationalize their need not to compete by falsely denying the importance of competition, success or failure, and therefore assiduously avoid competitive encounters.

- *The perpetual injury syndrome*
Another way that these athletes can avoid competition is by being perpetually injured during training. Such athletes have strong feelings of inferiority, but cannot simply opt out of the sport because of fear of isolation or rejection. Injury allows these 'training-room athletes' to avoid competition which they fear might expose their physical limits, but to remain a member of the team, thereby preserving their egos. In addition, injury allows them to live out the fantasy that, but for the injury, they would be exceptional athletes.

- *Fear of displacing idols*

Athletes who have used their idolization of former champions to motivate their performances may become anxious once they are in a position to challenge their heroes' or heroines' records.

- *The responsibility of being first or the champion*

Once an athlete sets a record, fans expect him or her to set records at each subsequent competition. In this way, fans develop unrealistically high expectations, with only perfection being acceptable. Thus, any performance below a record may be regarded with resentment. This can be a heavy burden on the athlete, who may fall short of ultimate performance because of these pressures.

The 'fear-of-success' syndrome is only one of many psychological causes of competitive failure. It illustrates the point that psychological factors can be crucial, and must be considered in competitive failures. If it is suspected that an athlete's perpetually poor performances are due to psychological factors, the help of the appropriate specialist should be sought.

The following two techniques relate to controlling pre-race arousal or tension through focusing the mind and body on relaxation. Although they form part of race preparation and are referred to in Chapter 9, they should be practised for months prior to racing, and should ideally form part of all athletes' training regimes.

Technique 6: Autogenic phrase training

Autogenic phrase training concentrates on your muscular and autonomic functions (e.g. heart and breathing rate) and on your mental state. To begin, you should lie in a relatively relaxed body position (preferably stretched out on your back). Now imagine that your limbs and abdominal area are growing 'warmer'. Once these areas have become 'warm', imagine them becoming 'heavier', and once this has been achieved, begin to repeat a personal autogenic phrase such as 'I feel strong, relaxed and confident'. This phrase should reflect your desired mental and physical arousal state.

Frequent repetition of this procedure establishes a conscious association between the desired arousal state and the autogenic phrases, so that when you repeat your personal autogenic phrases, the conditioned controlled arousal response is elicited. This technique can induce changes in muscle temperature, in heart and respiratory rates, and in the brain's electrical wave patterns.

Technique 7: Progressive relaxation

Progressive relaxation is a technique used to induce muscular relaxation and is particularly effective for people who have trouble falling asleep. Many athletes find that sleep is hard to come by the night before a race, and this technique could prove advantageous. To use progressive relaxation effectively, you contract and then relax your muscle groups, progressing from one muscle group to another, until the major muscle groups have been exercised. The reason for first contracting each muscle group is to teach you to appreciate what muscle tension feels like. Without conscious recognition of the two extreme sensations of muscle tension and relaxation, you will not be able to voluntarily induce the appropriate degree of muscle relaxation. Like all psychological techniques, progressive relaxation should be practised regularly for some months before a major competition, so that you acquire the appropriate proficiency by the time you need to use it.

Progressive relaxation should ideally be practised in a quiet, comfortable room that is free from distractions. The best place is usually the runner's bedroom, and this should be heated and carpeted with the lights dimmed or the curtains drawn. You should follow this five-step sequence:

- Lie on your back on the floor with your hands resting on or next to your abdomen, with legs extended and feet rotated outwards. Ensure that you are comfortable and then relax as much as you can.
- Next, clench your right fist and feel the sensation of tension in your right fist, hand and forearm. Try to be as specific as possible, so that you don't tense your jaw and neck at the same time.
- Then relax and feel the fingers of your right hand become loose. As you do so, contrast the feelings of muscle contraction and relaxation.
- Repeat this procedure, first with the right hand again, then with the left hand twice, and then with both hands together.

- Now repeat the same sequences for all the major muscle groups in the body, particularly the muscles of the face, neck, shoulders, upper back, chest, stomach, lower back, buttocks, hips, thighs and calves. Exercise all the muscle groups, taking care not to rush the sequence. At all times, carefully note the extent of the difference in the sensations of relaxation and contraction.

The complete sequence of progressive relaxation exercises should be practised three times a day for fifteen minutes, with the last session scheduled immediately before going to sleep. The beneficial effects of the procedure should become apparent within a few weeks. One modification of this technique which some have found helpful, is to begin the sequence of contraction and relaxation at the feet and work up to the head. You may also find the exercise more comfortable if your head is raised by a few centimetres, using a support, and by bending your knees with your feet flat on the ground. This flattens your back on the floor, placing less stress on your spine.

Those who have had lessons in the Alexander Technique, a discipline related to body posture and tension release, or who have practised yoga exercises, will learn this technique without difficulty.

The techniques outlined in this section could, if practised, lead to substantial improvements in performance. They do not, however, constitute the alpha and omega of psychological aspects of running. Runners who agree with these ideas, and who feel they could benefit, or have already benefitted from the application of some of these techniques, would obviously be advised to read more on the subject, and to seek the help of appropriately-trained professionals.

PSYCHOLOGICAL BENEFITS OF RUNNING

People have been known to excel in activities which give them little pleasure, but they tend to be exceptions to the rule. In general, we are more likely to succeed in those activities which reward us with both physical and psychological stimulation and satisfaction. Thus, if we are to do our best in any undertaking, it would be to our advantage to choose one which rewards us in this way. What are the physical and psychological rewards associated with running? As

*Running is fun!
Children can
teach us to
rediscover its
pleasures*

these are revealed to us, they can become incentives or motivating factors which can assist us in preparing to run our best.

Running is fun. We can tell this by watching any group of four-year-old children in a park. Apart from time spent on playground apparatus, most children's outdoor activity and play involves running, usually accompanied by shouts of hilarity. Running as recreation is as old as humankind, but the explosion of the sport as a favoured pastime of the masses is a relatively recent phenomenon, and appears to be associated with a world-wide concern for healthy living, coupled with an emphasis on appropriate diets and exercise. It is also associated with a growing realization of the importance of leisure and recreation in our lives. The appeal of running perhaps lies in its ability to transport us back to our childhood sense of freedom and joy in play.

For the uninitiated, the sight each year of thousands of runners in various stages of anguish, agony and despair forcing their obviously unwilling bodies through the 90 km Comrades Marathon might seem the very antithesis of play and freedom! While this may be true, a closer look at the faces of the same people as they cross the finish line will reveal deeper truths about running – its power to grant a sense of triumph, a boost in self-esteem, and a reinforcement of confidence which overflows to all facets of life.

For those who might demand more substantial proof than abstract psychological concepts, it has been shown that endurance athletes are generally health-conscious and follow good health practices. The potential long-term health benefits enjoyed by runners with these attitudes should not be dismissed lightly. For example, it has been shown that longevity and physical health are very strongly influenced by seven health practices typical of endurance athletes; avoiding smoking; taking regular exercise; eating moderately and controlling body weight; eating regularly; eating breakfast; drinking alcohol moderately or not at all and sleeping seven to eight hours per night. At the age of 45, a person who follows all seven health practices has a life expectancy that is some eleven years longer than someone the same age who follows three or less of these rules. By comparison, the greatest medical advances since the turn of this century have increased the longevity of men and women who reach the age of 45 by a mere four years.

On this basis, running, because of its strong association with the above health practices, is one of the most powerful health-tools we have ever known. In addition, running is linked to positive personality traits, and a variety of aspects of quality of life.

Personality

Studies have linked a range of positive personality traits with endurance exercise, and with running in particular. Whether running 'selects' people who display these traits, or whether these traits are enhanced in those who have chosen the sport is uncertain. Our belief is that it is the latter.

Evidence from various studies includes the findings that healthy adults who had exercised regularly for four or more

Running can add balance to your life and even improve you mood. These young athletes seem relaxed and cheerful

years exhibited greater energy, patience, humour, ambition, emotional stability, imagination, self-sufficiency, assurance and optimism, and were more amiable, graceful, good-tempered, elated and easy-going than a group of people who had just begun an exercise-training programme.

In addition, studies have shown that exercise training increases self-confidence, conscientiousness and persistence. Runners in particular have been found to be more introverted, stable, self-sufficient and imaginative than inactive persons, and also experienced low levels of anxiety, and enhanced self-esteem and body image.

It has been claimed that running can generate certain qualities, such as dependability, tenacity, organization, and the willingness to take risks and push to the limit, that have tremendous pay-offs in our society. Both the findings of science and our own experiences seem to bear this out.

Quality of life

Enhancing longevity alone may not be sufficient attraction for those considering embarking on an endurance exercise programme. It might be argued that it is not the length, but the quality of life that is important. These two aspects, however, are usually linked, and there is ample evidence associating running with enhanced quality of life.

Happiness has been found to be strongly associated with optimum physical fitness, and this correlates with the finding that anxiety levels are reduced after vigorous exercise. It is our experience that exercise, and specifically endurance running, has a specific effect on anxiety which is not duplicated by any other means. Exercise has also been found to be more effective than tranquillizers for reducing resting muscle tension.

Jogging has also proved an effective adjunct in the treatment of depression, and may be at least as effective (and considerably cheaper) as conventional drug therapy in cases of mild depression. In particular, exercise training has been found to be the most effective method of reducing depression caused by a stressful lifestyle.

In general, exercise greatly increases our ability to cope with stress and endurance-trained subjects in particular show a reduced physiological response to psychosocial stress. We have found that running enables us to cope more easily with the stress and discomfort of daily problems. It is as if running enables us to get our everyday problems into perspective.

Alternatively, it may be that the prior exercise alters the concentrations of certain chemical transmitters in the brain, including endorphins, and these then dampen our responses to stress. Endorphins themselves have been the subject of much study. These morphine-like substances are produced by the body itself as part of the normal response to stress. During running, the levels of endorphins in the body rise, and it has been argued that this is responsible for the euphoria ('runner's high') experienced by some athletes

A sense of humour is an important asset, especially when the competition is tough. Friends and rivals Elana Meyer and Tanya Peckham share a joke prior to a street mile in 1990

during running, as well as the calm that runners feel after exercise. Although findings are not conclusive, it seems that exercise plays a role in adapting the body's own chemistry for optimum mental health.

PSYCHOLOGICAL DANGERS OF TRAINING

Much of the argument that running is possibly detrimental to one's psychological health (mostly submitted by compulsive non-runners), is based on the accusation that running is 'addictive'. Those who follow this school of thought contend that running is associated with various abnormal psychological states, such as neuroticism, obsessive-compulsiveness, narcissism, masochism, and anorexic or addictive personalities.

It is beyond the scope of this book to debate the arguments for and against running addictions and their associated dangers. Suffice to say that there are pitfalls in many facets of life which in themselves are recognized as healthy and life-enriching. It is important that running is seen in a holistic context, as a part of our daily life rather than the essence of life itself. For some, running will be a major component, worthy of significant time investment. For others, it will be less so. It is important to examine our motives for running, and at all costs, to avoid the most dangerous of all running pitfalls – the Selfish Runner's Syndrome. (See Principle 20 in Chapter 4, p. 105.)

TRAINING THE MIND: conclusions

We have tried to demonstrate in this chapter the role of the mind in running your best, and to show that it is possible to improve mental attitudes towards competition, thereby improving running performance. We do not all aspire to world record status, but many of us would like to realize our full running potential. To do so we must train both the body and the mind, and it is the latter, perhaps the more elusive resource, which might ultimately determine our success. Roger Bannister recognised the wisdom of this when, two years after breaking through the four-minute-mile barrier, he wrote: 'Though physiology may indicate respiratory and cardiovascular limits to muscular effort, psychological and other factors beyond the ken of physiology set the razor's edge of defeat or victory and determine how closely the athlete approaches the absolute limits of performance'.

III

NUTRITION

8 NUTRITION:
The fuel source

We have looked at significant aspects of physical and mental training in Chapters 4 to 7. Before examining how best to harness this information in preparation for racing, we must next consider in some detail another component which can have a major bearing on running our best: nutrition.

We saw in Chapter 1 that, not unlike the internal combustion engine, the human body is dependent on appropriate fuel to run efficiently. Here we will discuss how to ensure that we fuel our bodies for optimum efficiency and so equip ourselves to run our best.

Three basic principles determine appropriate nutrition:

1. The body requires essential nutrients: these are the energy-supplying foods (carbohydrates, fats and proteins), and those nutrients necessary to assist the body to process and utilize that energy (vitamins, minerals, trace elements and water).
2. These nutrients are contained in four basic foodstuff groups: (i) the meat, fish, and meat-substitute group; (ii) the fruit and vegetable group; (iii) the milk and dairy group; and (iv) the bread and cereal group.
3. Food items from these four groups should be eaten in the following portions each day: groups i and iii: two portions a day; group ii: five portions a day; and group iv: four portions a day.

ENERGY-SUPPLYING FOODS

Carbohydrate is the primary energy source for the body. Because of this, exercise performance can be enhanced by increasing the intake of carbohydrate before exercise, reducing the rate at which those stores are burned during subsequent exercise, and by maintaining a high rate of carbohydrate utilization through consuming appropriate amounts of carbohydrates during exercise.

Fat is an alternative fuel source to carbohydrate. Fat stores are drawn upon as the carbohydrate stores become progressively depleted during prolonged exercise. However, because fats cannot be metabolized as fast as carbohydrate, it follows that exercise intensity must drop once carbohydrate stores are depleted.

Protein is important for structural development and repair of muscles, but has limited value as a fuel source.

The use or abuse of these different nutrients is a major determinant in achieving top athletic performance according to one's basic genetic potential.

Carbohydrates

Carbohydrates are known as the essential foodstuff for athletes, particularly distance runners. Pre-race 'carbo meals' have become an obligatory, almost ritualistic component of the marathon runner's lifestyle. In spite of all this, there is a surprising amount of ignorance about this foodstuff. What exactly are the best carbohydrate foods? How much carbohydrate should be eaten in training? How should one best carbo-load? Are there any pitfalls in this habit?

'Sugar and spice...': *the myth of carbohydrates*
The popular myth concerning high carbohydrate diets suitable for athletes is that one can indulge in all manner of cakes and confectionery without feeling guilty. The reverse is in fact true. Table 8.1 gives a list of foods with a high carbohydrate content, each comprising at least 90% carbohydrate, with less than 5% each of protein and fats. These foodstuffs, rather than sweets and cake, are the type which should be eaten during heavy training or when carbohydrate-loading before a racing event.

Table 8.1: High carbohydrate foods

potatoes	sugar	grapes	carrots
rice	honey	raisins	parsnips
macaroni	marmalade	oranges	artichokes
beetroot	jams	bananas	turnips
porridge	stewed fruit	prunes	fruit juices
crisp bread	white bread	molasses	

A high carbohydrate diet is one which consists almost exclusively of fruit, vegetables and cereals (bread, pasta, rice, potatoes, breakfast cereals). Chocolates, confectionery, and other carbohydrate sources may have a lower carbohydrate content in comparison because of their high fat content.

It is best to eat natural and unrefined forms of high-carbohydrate food, for example, potatoes, bread and rice when carbohydrate-loading, as these supply the B-vitamins essential for carbohydrate metabolism. Refined carbohydrates should not comprise more than 25% of the total carbohydrate intake.

What should the carbohydrate content of the diet be during heavy training?

Studies show that the muscles of athletes eating a normal mixed diet (that is, comprising 40% carbohydrate) show a progressive drop in muscle glycogen content when they exercise for up to two hours a day. This fall was somewhat averted, however, when the athletes ate a high carbohydrate diet (containing 70% carbohydrate). As depletion of muscle glycogen is one of the most important limiting factors in running your best over distances in excess of 30 km, or higher-intensity shorter bursts of exercise, the importance of following sound nutritional principles in preparing for races becomes apparent.

In practice, however, few athletes eat a diet that contains as much carbohydrate, largely because such diets can be extremely bland and unappetizing. Unfortunately, it is the protein and fat content of food that increases its palatability. Baked potatoes without butter and pasta without sauce lose much of their appeal!

An example of a balanced high carbohydrate diet (i.e. one that contains 70% carbohydrate) that can be followed during heavy training is given over the page in Table 8.2.

Carbo-loading: elite athlete Juliet Prowse with some of the essential ingredients for the pre-race diet

Table 8.2 Balanced high carbohydrate diet

orange juice	1 ℓ
skim milk	0,2 ℓ
wholewheat bread	10 slices
cereals or muesli	50 grams
bananas	3
apples	2
potatoes or pasta	200 g

To load or not to load: What is the answer?

(The 'carbohydrate-loading, carbohydrate-depletion' diet)

As we noted in Chapter 3, you can increase your body's capacity to store carbohydrate by training intensively. You can improve this capacity further by following a high carbohydrate diet during training. A reduction in your training load prior to a race will also increase your muscle glycogen levels. The next question is whether there are further benefits to be had by attempting to increase body carbohydrate stores by eating specific foods immediately prior to competition.

Carbohydrate-loading (known to runners as carbo-loading) refers to a process of boosting muscle glycogen levels immediately before competition, and is widely used by marathon runners. Studies have shown that carbohydrate-loading increases muscle glycogen levels from 14 g/kg to 21 g/kg in trained individuals. (It must be remembered that although the body can only store a fixed amount of carbohydrate, this amount varies between individuals and also varies greatly in the same person at different times.)

Can I benefit further by following an initial carbohydrate-depletion phase?

Various studies have monitored the responses of different subjects to variations in carbohydrate intake. It appears that if you are relatively untrained, your potential to store muscle glycogen is greatest following a three-day period of carbohydrate fasting (the depletion phase). However, trained athletes are able to store similar amounts of glycogen without following the three-day fast if they follow a high carbohydrate diet, i.e. one consisting of up to 560 g of carbohydrate per day. Eating more does not seem to be of any additional benefit.

Thus it would seem that highly trained athletes should not undergo a carbohydrate-depletion phase, but should rather ensure that they carbohydrate-load adequately before competing. They should also take care to ingest an adequate amount of carbohydrates during prolonged exercise, especially if the exercise lasts more than four hours. By avoiding the carbohydrate-depletion phase, they also avoid some of the potential dangers to which their highly trained state makes them vulnerable. This is especially true if they have been sharpening.

Less well-trained runners, because they are not as finely tuned, are less likely to be adversely affected by the carbohydrate-depletion phase than elite runners, and evidence indicates they could benefit from this phase.

For how long should I carbo-load and what foods should I eat?

To achieve best results, a three-day loading period is suggested. Simple, glucose-based carbohydrates can be eaten during the first day of the diet, before you switch to a diet rich in complex, unrefined (starch-based) carbohydrates, such as potatoes and bread. A trained athlete may be able to achieve total muscle glycogen repletion within 18 to 24 hours, if a carbohydrate intake of 25 g/hr is maintained.

How do you know you are eating sufficient carbohydrates when carbo-loading?

Probably the clearest sign that sufficient carbohydrate has been stored during the loading phase is an increase in body weight. For every 1 g of carbohydrate that is stored, it seems that approximately 2–3 g of water are also stored. If the body carbohydrate stores were completely empty before carbohydrate-loading commenced, body weight in a 70 kg male should increase by 2,0–2,5 kg (equivalent to a total carbohydrate store of 600 g) during the loading phase. The magnitude of this increase in weight will depend on body mass; obviously, it will be proportionally less in a 50 kg female.

To help you choose what to eat while carbo-loading, Table 8.3 lists the carbohydrate content in grams of various commonly eaten foodstuffs.

Table 8.3 Carbohydrate content of various foods

Food (100 g unless stated)	Carbohydrate content
Biscuit	65
Large chocolate milkshake	60
Cake with chocolate icing (150 g)	58
Chocolate bar	57
Brown bread	50
Breakfast cereal	43
Fruit mince pie	25
Macaroni or spaghetti	23
Banana	19
Baked potato	19
Apple	13
Unsweetened orange juice (100 ml)	11
Cola drink (200 ml)	11
Grapefruit	10
Peach	9

The safest way to carbo-load before a race is simply to modify the diet in the following ways:

- Eat cereals, bread (with honey), fruit and fruit juices for breakfast. Use skim milk in place of full cream milk, as it has a lower fat content.
- Substitute pasta (macaroni, spaghetti, etc.) for meat and eat more potatoes.
- If still hungry, eat sweets, but not to the point of gluttony.
- Supplement the diet with 200 g of a high-carbohydrate 'carbo-loading' athletic drink.

Are any other food supplements necessary while carbohydrate-loading?

Indications are that at least additional potassium, water, and vitamins should be taken when carbo-loading. Clearly, fluid intake needs to be increased during the loading phase so that sufficient water can be stored with the glycogen. The best guide to adequate fluid supplementation is urine colour. Urine that is pale in colour indicates an adequate fluid intake.

Potassium is also stored with glycogen and so with in-creased carbohydrate intake, potassium requirements increase. This need can best be met by eating oranges, tomatoes, bananas and potatoes – all good sources of both potassium and carbohydrate.

It is also probably beneficial to take a vitamin supplement while carbohydrate-loading; however, avoid taking vitamin B complex tablets during exercise, particularly those containing nicotinic acid. When present in high concentrations in the blood, nicotinic acid prevents the mobilization of free fatty acids. Thus if taken in high doses shortly (hours) before exercise, nicotinic acid will impair endurance performance by increasing the rate at which muscle glycogen is used during exercise.

Supplementing the diet with moderate to high doses of one or more of the anti-oxidant vitamins (beta-carotene, vitamin C and vitamin E) may reduce the risk of developing an infection before or after a marathon or ultramarathon race.

Are there any dangers in the carbo-loading diet?

Carbohydrate-loading does not suit everyone. While most will probably run better after loading, a few athletes may be adversely affected, and will no doubt curse the day they ever tried this diet.

The main risk in carbohydrate-loading is that very high concentrations of carbohydrate can cause intestinal distress, particularly diarrhoea, which may persist until the race. The second major problem of the diet, if one first undergoes the carbohydrate-depletion phase, is that physical performance capacity falls steeply during depletion. After a period of about 24 hours without carbohydrates, any physical effort beyond than a walk becomes very tiring. Worse still, after 36 hours of carbohydrate-depletion, even the most sunny-tempered and congenial runner becomes an irritable, aggressive, short-tempered monster. Thirdly, it seems that the long depletion run originally advocated by Scandinavian researchers (an original component of the depletion phase was a long, two-hour run at the outset of the phase, which had the effect of significantly reducing glycogen levels before even beginning the depletion diet), coming as it does only seven days before a major race must be detrimental. For this reason, it is probably better to run relatively short distances during the three days of carbohydrate-depletion, rather than doing one single long run.

There is no restriction to the number of times that carbohydrate-loading can be undertaken each year. The sole restriction is that it should not under any circumstances be

Not a recommended diet! Fats and oils, however, are an important part of the runner's diet. Vegetable oils are preferable to animal fats

tried for the first time before a major race, as the results will be disappointing for some. Furthermore, the diet should be gradually adapted to the individual's needs, and should not be followed blindly without modification. You should also remember that some runners do not respond well to the diet, and their performance will be worse rather than better when subsequently competing. Elite athletes are probably best advised to avoid the depletion phase altogether.

Carbohydrate intake during the race

We have looked at the importance of following a high carbohydrate diet during heavy training or prior to racing. What of our body's requirements during the race?

We have learnt in recent years that carbohydrate replacement is essential for optimal running performance, particularly for races which last for more than two hours. For races shorter than this period, fluid replacement remains more important, but a low percentage carbohydrate drink should nonetheless be taken. For races lasting more than 2 hours, drinks with higher percentages of carbohydrate should be taken. The type, quantity and composition of suitable fluids are described in Chapter 9 (see pp. 188–9).

Carbohydrate tips: a summary

Having established the important role of dietary carbohydrate in exercise performance, we can extract the following essential facts:

- The body has limited carbohydrate stores.
- These carbohydrate stores are utilized at rates proportional to the intensity of exercise.
- In the vast majority of athletes, the larger the carbohydrate stores before exercise, the better the performance. A diet of 70% carbohydrate is recommended when in heavy training or prior to racing.
- A high carbohydrate diet should consist almost exclusively of fruit, vegetables and cereals (bread, pasta, rice, potatoes and breakfast cereals), rather than sweets and other confectionary.
- The extent to which the body carbohydrate stores are filled depends on the carbohydrate content of the runner's regular diet, and can be increased by the 'carbohydrate-loading' diet.
- Less well-trained runners could benefit from a carbohydrate-depletion phase prior to loading, whereas highly trained athletes should avoid this phase.
- During the carbohydrate-loading diet, initially eat glucose-based carbohydrates before switching to complex, starch-based carbohydrates.
- Additional water, potassium and vitamins should be taken during the carbohydrate-loading diet.
- Don't use the carbohydrate-loading diet for the first time before an important race – it is not suitable for all runners and may have negative side effects.

Fats

Dietary fats have suffered bad press, which is not entirely deserved, as fats play an important role in exercise performance, particularly in prolonged exercise. Unfortunately, fats may cause health problems if eaten in excessive amounts over a long period of time.

What role do fats play in the supply of fuel?

Fats provide a convenient, palatable and highly concentrated source of energy, a source which becomes increasingly significant as the duration of exercise increases.

Although the oxidation of fat alone can sustain an exercise intensity of only about 50% VO_2 max, it has been found that after two hours of exercise at 65% VO_2 max, 50% or more of your energy may be derived from fat oxidation, pointing to its significance as a fuel in distance running.

What are the important foodstuffs containing fats and how much fat should we eat?

Foods rich in animal fat include butter and other full-cream dairy products such as full-cream milk, cream and hard cheese, meat, the visible fat of meat, the skin of chicken and egg yolk. Plant fats include polyunsaturated fats such as vegetable oils, salad dressings, and soft margarine and also monounsaturated fats, found in nuts, olives and avocados. While animal and plant fats provide the same amount of energy per gram, the former are more harmful to the body, as they increase the risk of coronary heart disease.

As an endurance athlete, fats should comprise about 15% of your total food intake.

Problems and dangers

The practical problems for the endurance athlete stem from the fact that fat, which has the highest energy source per gram if compared with protein and carbohydrate, generally comes hidden in the form of tempting treats, which often lead to over-indulgence. In addition, there is accumulating evidence that fat itself stimulates food intake, thereby promoting obesity. Compounding this is the fact that the body stores fat more efficiently than it does carbohydrate, so it is possible to eat too much fat before eating sufficient carbohydrates. This could be particularly problematic during 'carbohydrate-loading'. In addition, various health dangers are associated with a high fat diet:

- There is a relationship between the amount of animal fat in the diet, blood cholesterol levels, and the risk of developing coronary artery disease. A high intake of fat is related to high blood cholesterol levels, and an increased risk of this disease.
- The risk of cancer of the colon in both sexes, and breast cancer in women, is also increased in those who eat a high fat diet.
- Weight gain is far greater on a fat-rich diet than on an equicaloric carbohydrate-rich diet. The body has more

difficulty regulating its body fat content, especially in those who are genetically predisposed to weight gain because of a low capacity to use fat as a fuel. As a result, these individuals readily increase their body fat stores when eating a high fat diet.

Running and fat: a summary
The following points are significant with respect to the role of fats in the diet of distance athletes:

- During exercise, fats play an increasingly important role as a fuel, becoming a major fuel source after one-and-a-half to two hours of exercise at lower intensities. At higher intensities, carbohydrates remain the more important fuel for up to three hours.
- Fat is a high energy source which is stored more efficiently in your body than carbohydrates. It may create problems, however, by suppressing your appetite before you have eaten enough carbohydrate to restock your stores.
- Fat is associated with certain health risks.
- Those predisposed to put on weight do so most easily when partaking of a high fat diet.
- Despite all these negative factors, there is growing interest in the possibility that eating a high fat diet for a short period of up to three weeks may cause specific adaptations in muscle that can subsequently aid performance during exercise which lasts more than three hours, by sparing muscle glycogen stores.

Protein

There are few greater dietary myths than those surrounding the role of protein in the diet of those involved in vigorous exercise. Science has clearly shown that large helpings of eggs served with underdone steaks will have no direct influence on strength or endurance.

Protein plays a major role in the body, however, providing the basic structure of most body tissues and of hormones, cellular enzymes and genes. In all of these structures, proteins are in a dynamic state; that is, they are continually being broken down and replaced by new proteins which are absorbed from the gut. This continual protein replacement is known as the protein turnover rate and amounts to about 25 g of protein per day in a 70 kg male.

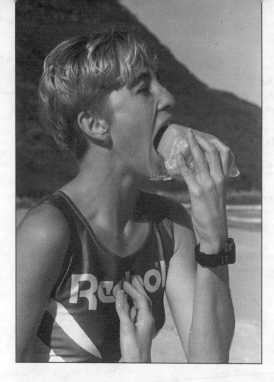

Cheese is a good source of protein, but should be one component in a balanced diet, not a meal in itself!

Protein plays a relatively minor role during exercise and only during prolonged exercise, once the carbohydrate stores have been depleted, does protein become more important. Even then, it supplies only about 10% of the total energy requirements, with most of the remainder coming from fats. Nevertheless, the increased use of proteins during and after exercise may be sufficient to justify increasing the daily protein intake of endurance runners to 18 g per kg per day – about twice that of inactive persons.

A variety of stresses such as physical training, severe illness, or major surgery all lead to an increased protein turnover rate. What is more, it seems likely that during the recovery stages after marathon and ultramarathon races, the rate of protein turnover is increased, partly to repair the muscle damage caused by such events. In these instances, the increased demand for protein is internally generated. Thus in spite of the myth which prevails, it is not possible to increase the body's protein metabolism artificially, and thereby stimulate muscle growth, simply by eating larger amounts of protein. Part of any excess protein intake will be converted to fat, while the remainder will be excreted by the kidneys.

Studies have shown in fact that excessively high protein diets are useless to the athlete. As the protein content of the diet increases, proportionately less is absorbed from the intestine for use in the body, and more of the protein breakdown products are excreted in the urine.

To sum up, protein is a valuable foodstuff in that it provides the basic structure of the muscle. It also plays an important role in repairing muscle damage, but it is of limited value as an energy food. It is impossible to stimulate muscle growth through eating high protein diets. However, eating too little protein will interfere with running performance and may predispose to other problems, including osteoporosis. In addition, high quality proteins contain all the essential amino acids that the body cannot manufacture itself. Animal proteins contain all the essential amino acids, but plant proteins lack one or more of these. Vegetarian athletes are therefore at risk of developing deficiencies of specific amino acids.

VITAMINS, MINERALS AND TRACE ELEMENTS

We have investigated the role of carbohydrates, fats and proteins in providing the fuel source for the body – the energy-giving substances. We turn now to those foodstuffs which play a vital role in the processes which convert that food energy into the body's energy currency, so that it can be utilized effectively – vitamins and trace elements.

Vitamins

The vitamins group consists of a set of unrelated organic compounds which, although needed only in minute quantities, are essential for specific metabolic reactions and for normal growth and development. Vitamins in fact regulate the metabolism, and are a vital part of the metabolic processes that convert fat and carbohydrate into energy. They also assist in the formation of bone and other tissues.

On a more practical level, the question as to whether people who are active in sports require an increased intake of vitamins often arises in running circles. There is actually very little evidence to support the practice of supplementing a nutritionally balanced diet with additional vitamins, even if exercise does possibly deplete certain vitamin stores such as riboflavin (vitamin B) and vitamin C. Vitamin deficiencies are extremely uncommon in athletes, with the possible exception of folate deficiency, and the only vitamin deficiencies that have been shown to impair performance are those of thiamine (vitamin B) and vitamin C. However, these deficiencies are essentially unknown in athletes. No study has yet shown that vitamin supplementation increases athletic performance in those who follow a normal diet.

However, one situation involving vitamins that is currently topical, is the consumption by some athletes of such high doses of vitamins that they no longer function in their usual role in the body, but act as drugs. This activity may in fact improve athletic performance in as yet undefined ways. However, nothing has been scientifically proven in this regard.

Nevertheless, there is evidence that very large doses of the antioxidant vitamins (beta-carotene or vitamin A, vitamin C and vitamin E) may reduce the risk of developing the infections and other free radical damage that are associated with very heavy training. Antioxidant vitamins may also reduce the risk of developing certain chronic diseases such as heart disease and cancer. It is possible that there may be additional, but as yet unrecognized chemicals in antioxidant foodstuffs that enhance or perhaps explain the beneficial effects currently ascribed to the antioxidant vitamins. However, the large doses required are more easily obtained from supplements rather than from the foods themselves.

Minerals and trace elements

The most important minerals in the diet include sodium, potassium, magnesium, calcium, iron, zinc and copper.

Table 8.4
Minerals required by the body

RDA = recommended dietary allowance; M = male; F = female

Classification	Mineral	RDA	Food sources
Macronutrients (essential at intakes of 100 mg or more per day)	Sodium	500 mg	Table salt, milk, meat, fish, poultry
	Potassium	2-4 g	Cereals, fruit and vegetables
	Magnesium	M 350 mg, F 300 mg	Cereals, legumes, nuts, meat, milk
	Calcium	800-1200 mg	Milk, cheese, ice cream, broccoli, oysters
	Chlorine		Table salt
	Sulphur		Eggs, meat, milk, cheese, nuts, legumes
	Phosphorus	800 mg	Milk, cheese, eggs, legumes, nuts, whole grain cereals

Sodium

Two myths have developed around the use of sodium chloride (salt). These are, firstly, that athletes need to increase their salt intake when they start training hard, and secondly, that salt is an important cure for or preventative against cramps. What role, then, does sodium play in the body?

Sodium plays a number of important physiological roles, among others, relating to water distribution and the regulation of blood pressure. It is stored mainly in the body's fluid, with a low concentration occurring inside the body's cells. The total sodium content of the body is about 80 g. Research has shown that people following a typical Western diet ingest between 10 and 12 g of salt daily. However, scientific evidence suggests that the body's daily salt requirement ranges from about 0,2 to 0,5 g, i.e. about one twentieth of what we actually consume. The excess salt is lost in the urine. Even vigorous and prolonged daily exercise increases salt requirements only very slightly, as sweat has a low salt content. In any case, as the runner grows fitter and better heat-acclimatized, sweating decreases.

In addition, the muscle cramps which develop during a single bout of prolonged exercise, such as an ultramarathon, are almost certainly not due to salt depletion, and are therefore unlikely to respond to salt ingestion. These cramps can be prevented only by a vigorous muscle stretching programme, and not by increasing one's intake of salt, magnesium or calcium.

While there is no published evidence of a salt deficiency ever having occurred in an athlete following a normal diet, even when exercise has been vigorous and air temperatures high, there is a possibility that a high salt intake may increase the risk of high blood pressure (hypertension), especially in individuals who are genetically prone to this condition. For this reason, most nutritional authorities advise a daily salt intake of no more than 3 g.

Where does this leave the runner? You are in the fortunate position that your chosen form of exercise rids you of some of the excess salt in your diet, and may therefore protect you against the development of high blood pressure.

Potassium

The major importance to runners of potassium is that it is stored with glycogen in the body; this means that extra potassium is required when the intake of carbohydrates is

Bananas and citrus fruits are good sources of potassium, especially important during carbo-loading

increased during carbo-loading. By eating citrus fruits, bananas and tomatoes (dietary sources of potassium) during carbohydrate-loading, you will adequately cover your additional potassium needs.

The daily potassium requirement is about 2–4 g, i.e. about four to eight times more than the daily salt requirement. The total body potassium store is about 90 g. During and after exercise, potassium is lost in urine and sweat, but these losses are negligible, and there is no evidence of any athlete ever having developed a potassium deficiency.

Magnesium

Low levels of soil magnesium are characteristic of large areas of South Africa. Levels in drinking and irrigation water are thus correspondingly low. If you live in one of these areas, you may well have a mild magnesium deficiency. Blood magnesium levels in South African runners are usually in the 'low normal' range, but it is uncertain whether their performance would improve if they increased their magnesium intake. It is worth noting however, that magnesium levels appear to be lowest in individuals with the highest VO_2 max values, suggesting that low blood magnesium levels may not be altogether bad.

Magnesium losses in urine and sweat are, like those of potassium, trivial. Thus the cause of any magnesium deficiency in athletes is almost certainly an inadequate dietary intake, rather than excessive sweat or urine losses. Meanwhile, studies of South African runners have failed to show evidence of magnesium deficiency, or any benefit from magnesium ingestion. Muscle magnesium levels – the major site of magnesium storage in the body – were in the normal range, and did not increase when the athletes took magnesium supplements.

Calcium

Most of the body's calcium is stored in bone; thus the major complication of calcium deficiency is reduced bone strength, due to inadequate bone calcification.

Women and those following an abnormal diet low in diary produce are the most likely to be at risk of calcium deficiency. Women who do not menstruate are at high risk for the development of osteoporosis (weakening of the bone tissue). They should increase their calcium intake by eating calcium-rich foods (dairy produce in particular), and should also seek the advice of a gynaecologist about whether they

Women runners in particular need to ensure an adequate level of calcium in their diet. Dairy products are a good source

are suitable candidates for hormone replacement therapy with the female hormones oestrogen and progesterone.

Supplementation should be with calcium carbonate or calcium citrate. Calcium absorption from these tablets is reduced by diets that are high in fibre and caffeine.

Iron

Of all the nutrient deficiencies in runners, anaemia due to low body stores of iron has received the most attention. A true iron-deficiency anaemia, in which the blood haemoglobin content is reduced, has a markedly negative effect on running performance. However, there is no evidence that low blood iron (ferritin) levels without evidence of anaemia (shown by low blood haemoglobin) influence performance, are a reliable indication of low body iron stores, or require treatment. In fact, low blood ferritin levels are associated with a reduced incidence of heart disease.

Women, however, are especially at risk of iron deficiency anaemia because the daily intake of iron in females is only marginally above the critical limit which is sufficient to balance normal daily iron losses. Additional iron losses caused by running may be sufficient to cause iron deficiency.

High-risk persons

You are a good candidate for anaemia if you:

- run high weekly mileages;
- are a woman runner who regularly experiences a heavy menstrual flow;
- follow a diet lacking in iron-rich foods such as liver, red meat, egg yolk, legumes, dark green leafy vegetables, molasses and whole grains;
- are a lacto-vegetarian (someone who eats no meat or eggs) or vegan (someone who does not eat any foods of animal origin, including dairy products).

Daily requirements

Daily iron requirements in heavily-training runners might be as much as 2 mg, but as only 10–15% of iron from non-animal sources (e.g. vegetables cooked in a cast-iron pot) and 40% of iron from animal sources (e.g. meat) is actually absorbed by the body, this means that you should aim to ingest about 20 mg iron per day. Daily iron losses should be balanced by a normal diet (which provides about 18 mg iron per day), but problems arise when the daily dietary intake is restricted or the daily iron losses exceed 2 mg. There is evidence that the diets of many elite women runners may yield only 9 mg iron per day.

Avoiding iron deficiency
If you border on iron deficiency, you would benefit by eating more red meat, the dark meat of fowls, or liver. Iron is best absorbed when taken with vitamin C. Simply by drinking fresh orange juice instead of tannin-containing teas, or eating an orange with meals, you can increase the iron absorption from your meal five-fold. Similarly, animal protein increases iron absorption from beans and peas.

Treatment
Iron therapy should be considered only if you are found to have iron-deficiency anaemia, i.e. a low blood haemoglobin content. Total body iron stores are between 3–5 g, so on a supplement of 200 mg elemental iron per day (and assuming 10% absorption), you would take between 150 and 250 days (5–8 months) to replenish your iron stores if your diet remains unaltered.

Zinc
The possibility that distance runners may be zinc-deficient has been raised by a recent study, in which blood zinc levels were found to be low in a group of runners and lowest in those who trained the hardest. The symptoms of zinc deficiency are fairly non-specific (loss of taste and smell, loss of appetite, loss of hair and skin lesions).

It is not known whether zinc deficiency adversely affects running performance, although one study has shown increased muscle strength and endurance after zinc supplementation. It should be noted that zinc is found mainly in protein foods, and its content is low in high-carbohydrate foods such as fruit, pastry, pasta and ice-cream. Vegetarian or vegan runners are thus more likely to experience zinc deficiency.

Copper, chromium and other trace elements
There is no published evidence of copper, chromium or trace element deficiencies in runners, even though exercise alters the metabolism of these elements and increases their losses in sweat, urine and faeces.

FINAL DIETARY POINTERS

The best diet for endurance athletes should contain 55–70% carbohydrate, 15–30% fat and 15% protein. Ideally, 350 to 500 g of carbohydrate should be eaten daily. Other pointers to a healthy diet which runners would do well to heed include the following:

- Eat a variety of foods.
- Reduce sucrose (table sugar) to 25% of total carbo-hydrate intake.
- Reduce fat consumption and substitute monounsaturated fats with polyunsaturated fats where possible.
- Reduce consumption of cholesterol to less than 300 mg/day.
- Limit salt intake to 5 g/day.
- Eat more high-fibre foods such as cereals, fruit and vegetables.
- Eat foods rich in vitamins A, C and E.
- Eat cruciferous vegetables (cabbage, broccoli and cauli-flower).
- Limit alcohol consumption.
- Limit consumption of salt-cured or smoked foods.

IV
RACING

9 RACING

Much of this book has focused on various aspects of training with a view to running your best. We do not suggest for one moment that competitive running is the only legitimate means of participating in the sport of distance running, and we have described in Chapter 7 the psychological and physiological benefits to be gained through simply running in relaxed fashion, particularly in an inspiring environment.

But for those who want to test the limits of their ability as a runner, racing against a measurable standard (usually time and/or other runners) has become the accepted way to do so. The earlier chapters on various aspects of training will have helped you to harness your running talents. Now you must prepare to race.

Make sure that you do justice to your ability by preparing as thoroughly as possible for your race. What follows are guidelines for racing which will help you to put together a pre-race programme which best suits you.

PHYSICAL PREPARATION

Many of the salient issues concerning the physical preparation for racing have been discussed in the earlier chapters. In particular, the 21 Principles of Running Your Best in Chapter 4 will equip you for most racing eventualities. We do not intend to repeat those sections here, but will refer to those aspects most relevant to racing. In addition, we will discuss various practical issues which will help you to focus all your energy on running your best.

Four months to three weeks before race day

Plan and incorporate sensible base and race-specific programmes into your training schedules

We have stressed that no single magical programme exists which will produce best results for all runners for all occasions. By incorporating the 21 Principles into your training lifestyle, you will be well on your way to gaining the most from running, both as a pastime and as a supreme test of your physical ability. By putting Principle 7 into practice (plan medium- and long-term programmes which incorporate specific, but non-exclusive phases), you will be including certain important aspects of training into your programme which will eventually enable you to race to the best of your ability. These aspects are:

- *Endurance:* a solid base programme of mainly aerobic running in order to enable you to accommodate the increased load of race-specific programmes;
- *Power:* specific sessions, such as fartlek and hill running are vital for survival towards the end of longer races, particularly on hilly courses, and for the ability to cope with pace changes during racing;
- *Speed:* sharpening your training with speed sessions will give you an important edge on race day.

Apply the essentials of peaking

This echoes Principle 14 for Running Your Best, and is of such significance for those who wish to race at their best, that it is worth repeating the most relevant aspects here.

- Only begin sharpening for a specific race after a solid base endurance programme. This is crucial; short cuts are invariably counterproductive.
- Combine various techniques of speed training into a peaking programme which includes fartlek, intervals, time trials and short races.
- Restrict speed or high quality training to a maximum of three sessions per week.
- Beware of doing too many high-intensity sessions and thus straying into overtraining territory (see pp. 71–5).

Acclimatize

The effects of altitude, weather, and time of day of the race on running performance were discussed in Chapter 2. Wherever possible, you should prepare yourself by training in similar conditions to those in which you expect the race to be run. This is particularly important in the final weeks leading up to the race.

If the race is at altitude, your best preparation is to have lived at altitude for many years. If you live at low altitude,

Racing: the ultimate test

the following options, in order of preference, are open to you:

- train at an altitude similar or higher to that of the race venue for a period of between one to three months prior to the race;
- arrive at the race venue at least three weeks prior to the race;
- arrive at the race venue as close as possible to the starting time of the race. It would appear that coastal athletes who arrive at altitude only a couple of hours prior to racing are less affected by the altitude than those who have arrived a few days before the race.

If the race is expected to be run in warm conditions, you should train in similar temperatures (or, if this is not possible, in a tracksuit), and at the same time of day as the race. You should follow these measures for a period of one to two weeks during the final month leading up to the race.

Three weeks before race day

Ensure that you undergo an adequate taper

We have learned that high-intensity tapers (described in Chapter 4 under Principle 15) are likely to prove superior to 'rest or jog' tapers in preparation for racing most distances, with the possible exception of the ultramarathon. Failure to allow sufficient time for tapering or to sufficiently reduce training volumes will mean that you are likely to arrive at the race short of your peak.

Although there are various schools of thought about how much to taper, a general rule is to reduce your training distance by 15 to 20 percent in the third week before a race, and a further 10 to 15 percent in the second week. The first three days of the final week should constitute only 40 percent of the usual training volume for those days, with the final days given to easy jogging over distances of up to 8 km, with one or two shortened quality sessions included. Alternatively, structure the final five days so that you taper from five intervals of 1 000 m to one such interval the day before the race. If time allows, three-week tapers are recommended.

This tapering schedule holds for distances between 21 km and 42 km. The taper should probably be increased (to about four weeks) for ultramarathons and reduced (to about one to two weeks) for 10 to 15 km races, or track and cross-country races. Also remember that the taper should involve a reduction in volume and not intensity, as we have previously discussed, and should include short time trials or intervals of 500 m to 2 000 m. The number of repetitions of the interval sessions, rather than the speed at which they are run, should be progressively reduced during the taper.

We have included a two week taper in our suggested programme for an elite 10 km race, and a three week taper in the programme for an elite marathon. (See Appendix 2, pp. 219 and 225.)

One week before race day

Carbohydrate-load prior to the race

The scientific rationale for carbohydrate-loading was described in Chapter 8, and sample diets for the loading phases were given. There is little doubt that a high carbohydrate diet prior to racing is beneficial, particularly if the race distance exceeds 20 km, but there is uncertainty as to

Two of the toughest racers in the business: Zola Pieterse and Elana Meyer neck-and-neck in a half marathon

the benefit of depleting your carbohydrate reserves immediately prior to the loading phase.

The loading phase should ideally take place only during the final three days before the race, during which mainly complex carbohydrates should be eaten. The amount of carbohydrate eaten each day during the loading phase should be about 500 to 600 g, some of which should be taken in liquid form.

Arrive at the race venue at the appropriate time

If the race is to be held out of town and not at high altitude (in which case follow the guidelines described on p. 176 above), the following rules apply:

- Arrive at least two days before the race and allow one day of recovery for each day spent driving there;
- Allow one day of recovery for each three hours spent flying there;
- If the competition is very far away, so that travelling involves crossing one or more time zones, allow one day of recovery for each time-zone crossed, in addition to the time allocated to recover from travelling itself.

Organize accommodation

Arrange your travel and accommodation so that all unfamiliar events and sights are reduced to a minimum, and as many minor frustrations as possible are avoided. Do not assume that out-of-town accommodation will be suitable. Check in advance that your room is comfortable, free from noise and relatively close to the race start. Enquire about the availability of any special foods that you will require (for example, for your high carbohydrate diet) as well as other facilities, such as saunas and swimming pools, that you may need for your comfort.

If you find it difficult to sleep in unfamiliar surroundings, take along some personal possessions such as photographs, and perhaps even your own pillow and bedclothes.

The day before the race

Drive over the course

Even if you know the course well, this is always a good tactic. It is particularly important to drive over the last section of the race. As this is a very specific part of your mental preparation, we describe this part of your pre-race tactics in the second half of this chapter.

Eat correctly

A disconcerting experience for any runner is to have their race interrupted by an unscheduled 'pit stop'. The emotion of the moment combined with a few hours of hard running will shake loose even the most resolute bowels. One way of avoiding such pit stops is to ensure that the intestine is empty before the race. This can be achieved by eating only highly-refined, low-bulk carbohydrate foods which leave little residue (white bread, cookies, sweets, rice, potatoes) for the last 16 to 24 hours before the race. (Do not under any circumstances resort to laxatives prior to the race.)

A relatively high percentage of runners appear to have mild forms of milk (lactose) or other food intolerances. By avoiding milk or other dairy produce for the last twenty-four hours before competing, you can limit or prevent this form of gastrointestinal disturbance.

Select and assemble your running gear

By laying out your running gear the night before and ensuring that you have everything you will need ready to hand, you can prevent any last-minute morning panic, which saps vital physical and mental energy, and which is characteristic of those unwise runners who neglect this step.

Pin your race numbers to your vest and drape the vest on a chair near to your bed. Pack a tog bag with petroleum jelly (to apply to those parts of the body liable to chafe), hairbands or clips (if necessary), toilet paper (sufficient for one or two pit stops and sealed in a water-proof packet), extra safety pins, any food supplements you require during the race, and a snack for after the race. It is useful to pack a change of clothing for after the race, including a change of shoes. If you are unsure whether or not water will be provided at the start of the race, also pack a bottle of water, which should preferably be kept in the fridge until you leave for the race.

The problems associated with controlling body heat and the limitations of clothing have been discussed in Chapters 1 and 2. Unless the race is likely to take place in temperatures below 15°C, or if the weather forecast predicts that a strong wind will be blowing, running pants and vests should be lightweight and porous, and will be all the clothing that is necessary. The best racing vests are of the nylon 'fish net' variety. When conditions are likely to be cold or wet, more than one layer of clothing should be worn, the arms should be covered, and every attempt should be made to stay as dry as possible. Wind combined with cold, wet conditions can bring on hypothermia, and in this case rain-proof clothing should be worn, at least over the upper body. This is especially important if the race is one which will last for more than a few hours.

For a detailed discussion on running shoes, consult *Lore of Running* or *Running Injuries*. Briefly, the shoes you choose to race in should be sufficiently worn-in to be comfortable, but not so old as to be worn-out. One absolutely unbreakable rule is never to run a long race in a pair of shoes you have

Xolile Yawa's mid-race surges have broken many an athlete, and helped him win the 1993 Berlin marathon. Here he kicks away from Lawrence Peu in a national championship

not previously used in one or more long training runs. Socks are useful in curbing blisters in longer-distance races, particularly if you first apply Vaseline to your feet.

Sacrificing support and cushioning for lighter weight could lead to a saving in the energy cost of running of up to 3%, but at the cost of sore feet, added stress on the musculo-skeletal system, and a greater chance of injury. The novice runner, unused to the stress of marathon running, is advised to run in a comfortable, more sturdy training shoe.

Get sufficient rest

Sacrificing sleep in your race build-up can be costly. As you are nearing your peak, your body needs sufficient rest to cope with the additional physical stresses placed on it. To short-circuit your body's natural recovery process is to invite illness and injury. As many runners find it difficult to sleep well the night before an important race, it is especially important to go to bed very early on the second last night before the race and sleep for as many hours as possible.

Sleep the night before the race is likely to be broken and disrupted, and you may find it useful to employ the progressive relaxation technique described in Chapter 7. Another means of relaxing is to imagine, in as much detail as possible, a tranquil place and to attempt to use your five senses to experience its peace and beauty. However, even when using these techniques, it is unusual for an athlete to sleep very deeply the night before a major race. This should not cause concern if you have rested well during the previous week. The night before the race your mind will be restless as it prepares for what lies ahead. If you sleep too deeply, it could indicate that you are not properly psyched up for the race.

Sex the night before? In spite of old ideas about 'involuntary losses during sleep being so weakening as to defeat all the trainer's best endeavours' (according to one H. Andrews writing on running and health at the turn of the century), it is currently believed that sexual activity (in moderation, of course) has no effect whatsoever on running performance.

The race day itself

Wake up gently

Studies have shown that correct waking procedures can have a positive effect in determining how the athlete will feel and perform during the rest of the day. As far as possible, follow these guidelines:

- You should be gently awakened by a clock-radio, or preferably by a quiet tap on your door. Avoid the use of a shrill alarm clock.
- Enjoy your favourite morning drink while getting up slowly and calmly.
- Repeat positive statements about how well you feel, and what a lovely day it is.
- Smile and get yourself into a relatively relaxed frame of mind while going through stretching and deep-breathing exercises.
- Get dressed while continuing to repeat positive self-statements.
- Try not to think about the race yet, as this will produce anxiety and high levels of arousal too soon before the competition itself.

Attend to final preparations

Your final pre-race preparations include applying Vaseline to those areas of the body that are liable to chafe, in particular the groin; cutting your toe-nails; and for men, who lack the protection of a bra, applying plasters to your nipples to prevent the chafing discomfort of 'jogger's nipples'.

Eat an appropriate pre-race breakfast

Not surprisingly, your pre-race breakfast can influence your performance on the road. Although virtually all of your energy requirements for the marathon have already been stored after three days of carbohydrate-loading, it is important to re-stock the glycogen stores in the liver which will have been depleted by about 50 g after an overnight fast. For the marathon, it is essential to maintain optimum liver carbohydrate stores if blood glucose levels are to be maintained towards the end of the race. Liver glycogen stores are adequate to prevent hypoglycaemia developing during races of less than 21 km. It may be counter-productive to eat breakfast before a 10 km, 15 km or even a 21 km race.

The pre-marathon breakfast should contain easily-digestible carbohydrates (bread, cornflakes, sugar, honey) and must be eaten at least two or three hours before the race starts. If you eat within one hour of the race, you will stimulate the release of the hormone insulin, which will mean that you will burn carbohydrates more rapidly than normal, and thus have an earlier encounter with 'the wall'.

It was originally thought that the 200 mg of caffeine contained in two cups of coffee primed the body for prolonged exercise by stimulating the release of those body hormones which mobilize free fatty acids from fat tissue. More recent evidence suggests that caffeine offers no such metabolic advantage, at least not in runners who have carbo-loaded and eaten breakfast. Nevertheless, even low doses of caffeine, equivalent to one or two cups of tea or coffee, do aid performance, probably as a result of caffeine's properties as a mental stimulant.

If you are in a position to eat a meal four to five hours before the race, there is evidence to suggest that a fatty meal (steak, eggs, bacon, milk, etc.) with some carbohydrate (cereal, bread and honey) may be of greater benefit than eating carbohydrates alone. This is because the fatty meal would cause blood levels of free fatty acid to rise, and could therefore have a carbohydrate-sparing effect.

Prepare for the start

We have already cautioned about the dangers of becoming caught up in the pre-race 'brag session' about how much training each athlete has done. Either time your arrival so that there is only enough time to check in and line up (having carried out your stretching and warm-up preparations elsewhere) or arrive early, check in, and isolate yourself to warm up and do stretching exercises. The warm-up should consist of slow jogging for five to fifteen minutes, with a few bursts at race pace, while stretching is important to overcome overnight residual stiffness in the calves, hamstrings and back muscles.

Five minutes before the start, drink 200 to 300 ml of cold fluid, either water or the carbohydrate-containing solution you plan to drink on the run. This will delay the onset of dehydration during the race.

We have described the dangers of racing in warm conditions. You should take the 'starting-line test' (see p. 47.) If you do not feel cold at the start in your skimpy running kit, adjust your time schedule accordingly and run at a slower pace, running for position rather than for a fast time. Although heat is likely to have a more adverse effect on performance over the marathon distance than in shorter races, only sprinters (up to 400 m) are likely to escape the heat with their performances unaffected, and you should adopt a cautious approach even for 10 km and 15 km races.

You have spent long hours preparing for your big race. Many runners, novices in particular, have a tendency to underperform due to a failure to translate their careful preparation into a race worthy of their efforts. An experienced racer who may be vastly undertrained can outperform a much fitter novice on race day, simply because of a superior understanding of the principles of racing, notably those of correct pacing.

There are essentially three ways to run a race: according to your body; your watch; or your heart rate. When running according to your body, you monitor effort; when running according to your watch, you monitor pace. If you have a pulse rate monitor, you can run according to a predetermined heart rate.

For the first few races, it is best to run according to your body, and to start every race at a pace that is slow enough for you to be certain of maintaining for the entire distance. It is disastrous to start too fast in any race, but especially so in

Talented athlete Eric Mhlongo is known for his courageous, but often ill-advised fast pace at the start of races. More often than not, this has cost him success in road races

your first longer race. Bitter experience has shown that any time you gain in this way in the first half of any race, is paid for twice over in the second half.

The golden rule is that the effort for both halves of the race must be nearly as equal as possible. Ignore those who insist that you should run the first half of any race faster so that you will have spare time to cushion your reduced pace in the second half. In reality, the fast early pace is the very reason for the fade in the second half. An advantage of running the second half of the race slightly faster than the first, is that if you can speed up when others are slowing down, you will get a mental lift from the impression that you are running much faster than you really are.

Table 9.1
Performance ratings for predicted equivalent running times over different racing distances

Performance rating*	Distance							
	1 mile	5 km	8 km	10 km	16 km	21,1 km	32 km	42,2 km
2000	3;34	12:00	20:53	26:43	44:25	59:53	1:33:28	2:05:52
1960	3:54	13:00	22:22	28:35	47:24	1:03:49	1:39:24	2:13:44
1910	4:18	14:00	24:02	30:39	50:42	1:08:11	1:46:03	2:22:29
1870	4:36	15:00	25:46	32:50	54:11	1:12:46	1:53:01	2:31:39
1830	4:54	16:00	27:26	34:54	57:30	1:18:08	1:17:38	2:40:24
1780	5:17	17:00	29:10	37:05	1:00:59	1:21:44	2:06:36	2:49:35
1740	5:34	18:00	30:44	39:03	1:04:08	1:25:53	2:12:54	2:57:53
1690	5:57	19:00	32:19	41:01	1:07:17	1:30:02	2:19:12	3:06:11
1650	6:15	20:00	34:08	43:18	1:10:55	1:34:50	2:26:29	3:15:48
1600	6:38	21:00	35:48	45:22	1:14:14	1:39:13	2:33:07	3:24:32
1560	6:55	22:00	37:27	47:26	1:17:33	1:43:35	2:39:45	3:33:17
1510	7:19	23:00	39:06	49:30	1:20:52	1:47:57	2:46:22	3:42:01
1470	7:37	24:00	40:46	51:35	1:24:11	1:52:19	2:53:00	3:50:46
1420	7:50	25:00	42:25	53:39	1:27:30	1:56:42	2:59:38	3:59:30
1380	8:07	26:00	44:05	55:43	1:30:48	2:01:04	3:06:15	4:08:15
1330	8:31	27:00	45:44	57:47	1:34:07	2:05:26	3:12:53	4:17:00
1290	8:49	28:00	47:24	59:52	1:37:26	2:09:48	3:19:31	4:25:44
1240	9:12	29:00	49:03	1:01:45	2:14:19	3:26:08	4:34:28	
1200	9:29	30:00	50:42	1:04:00	2:18:33	3:32:46	4:43:13	

*The performance rating is calculated as the year in which world records for the listed distances will equal the times given.

© 1978 T. Osler. Adapted with permission

It is important to gain some idea of how fast you are likely to run your marathon, and this is best done by racing sub-marathon distances prior to attempting the marathon. Table 9.1 gives predicted marathon times on the basis of times set over shorter distances. This knowledge will enable you to calculate an optimum pace for the marathon and may spare you some of the pain of 'blowing' through having started at too fast a pace. Table 9.2 provides schedules for standard marathons at paces varying from world-record pace to a seven-hour marathon.

Table 9.2
Pacing schedules for the standard marathon

Distance (km)	1	8	10	16	21,1	32	42,2
Time	3:00	24:00	30:00	48:00	1:03:18	1:36:00	2:06:36
	3:10	25:22	31:42	50:43	1:06:53	1:41:26	2:13:46
	3:20	26:38	33:18	53:17	1:10:16	1:46:34	2:20:32
	3:30	28:00	35:00	56:00	1:13:51	1:52:00	2:27:42
	3:40	29:22	36:42	58:43	1:17:26	1:57:26	2:34:52
	3:50	30:38	38:18	1:01:17	1:20:49	2:02:34	2:41:38
	4:00	32:00	40:00	1:04:00	1:24:24	2:08:00	2:48:48
	4:10	33:22	41:42	1:06:43	1:27:59	2:13:26	2:55:58
	4:20	34:38	43:18	1:09:17	1:31:22	2:18:34	3:02:44
	4:30	36:00	45:00	1:12:00	1:34:27	2:24:00	3:09:54
	4:40	37:22	46:42	1:14:43	1:38:32	2:29:26	3:17:04
	4:50	38:38	48:18	1:17:17	1:41:25	2:34:34	3:23:50
	5:00	40:00	50:00	1:20:00	1:45:30	2:40:00	3:31:00
	5:10	41:22	51:42	1:22:43	1:49:05	2:45:26	3:38:10
	5:20	42:38	53:18	1:25:17	1:52:28	2:50:34	3:44:56
	5:30	44:00	50:00	1:28:00	1:56:03	2:56:00	3:52:06
	5:40	45:22	56:42	1:30:43	1:59:08	3:01:26	3:59:16
	5:50	46:38	58:18	1:33:17	2:03:01	3:06:34	4:06:02
	6:00	48:00	1:00:00	1:36:00	2:06:36	3:12:00	4:13:12
	6:10	49:22	1:01:42	1:38:43	2:10:11	3:17:26	4:20:22
	6:20	50:38	1:03:18	1:41:17	2:13:34	3:22:34	4:27:08
	6:30	52:00	1:05:00	1:44:00	2:17:09	3:28:00	4:34:18
	6:40	53:22	1:06:42	1:46:43	2:20:44	3:33:26	4:41:28
	6:50	54:38	1:08:18	1:49:17	2:24:07	3:38:34	4:48:14
	7:00	56:00	1:10:00	1:52:00	2:27:42	3:44:00	3:55:24
	7:10	57:22	1:11:42	1:54:43	2:31:17	3:47:26	5:02:34
	7:20	58:38	1:13:18	1:57:17	2:34:10	3:54:34	5:09:20
	7:30	1:00:00	1:15:00	2:00:00	2:38:15	4:00:00	5:16:30
	7:40	1:01:22	1:16:42	2:02:43	2:41:20	4:05:26	5:23:40
	7:50	1:02:38	1:18:18	2:05:17	2:45:13	4:10:34	5:30:26
	8:00	1:04:00	1:20:00	2:08:00	2:48:48	4:16:00	5:37:36
	8:10	1:05:22	1:21:42	2:10:43	2:52:23	4:21:26	5:44:46
	8:20	1:06:38	1:23:18	2:13:17	2:55:16	4:26:34	5:51:32
	8:30	1:08:00	1:25:00	2:16:00	2:59:21	4:32:00	5:58:42
	8:40	1:09:22	1:26:42	2:18:43	3:02:56	4:37:26	6:05:52
	8:50	1:10:38	1:28:18	2:21:17	3:06:19	4:42:34	6:12:38
	9:00	1:12:00	1:30:00	2:24:00	3:09:54	4:48:00	6:19:48
	9:10	1:13:22	1:31:42	2:26:43	3:13:59	4:53:26	6:26:58
	9:20	1:14:38	1:33:18	2:29:17	3:16:22	4:58:34	6:33:44
	9:30	1:16:30	1:35:00	2:32:00	3:20:27	5:04:00	6:40:54
	9:40	1:17:22	1:36:42	2:34:43	3:24:02	5:09:26	6:48:04
	9:50	1:18:38	1:38:18	2:37:17	3:27:25	5:14:34	6:54:50
	10:00	1:20:00	1:40:00	2:40:00	3:31:00	5:20:00	7:02:00

Having established an appropriate pace at which to run your race, whether it be 10 km or the marathon, observe the following race tips to enable you to run your best on the day:

- Run with a digital watch which you should start when you cross the starting line (this may be after the start of the race);
- Check your pace over the first kilometre. If it is far too fast (as is likely in the case of novices), slow down drastically to ensure that your 3 km time is on schedule.
- If, in a marathon, your 3 km pace is still substantially too fast, walk. This will enable you to restart at the appropriate pace. Any time you lose in walking will be gained towards the end of the race, if you run the remaining distance according to your schedule. Beyond 3 km, if the pace is still too fast, it is unlikely that you will be able to repair the damage. For sub-marathon races, you may escape 'blow-out' by merely slowing your pace rather than walking, but you should still try to get onto your original schedule as soon as possible.
- Especially in windy conditions, it is beneficial to run in a group of runners with whose pace you feel comfortable. If you know there are experienced runners in the pack whose schedules are similar to yours, you should try to maintain contact with them for as long as possible. Only if you notice that your times are much faster than you had planned for, should you drop off the 'bus'.
- Your drinks should be as cold as possible, and your first one should be taken after 3 km. Thereafter, you should drink a total of about 500 ml/hour or a little more if you weigh more than 50–60 kg. If you are running at speeds approaching three minutes per kilometre, or running at temperatures in excess of 20°C, you should also increase your intake, to approximately 700 to 800 ml/hr. However, don't drink too much; you should limit yourself to a maximum intake of about 800 ml/hr.
- Sponging is a useful technique which assists in ridding your body of surplus heat; make use of it at every opportunity.
- If you are running a race in excess of 30 km or two hours duration, it is important that you take a carbohydrate-containing drink (containing glucose polymers, starch, maltose or sucrose, but not fructose, which can cause intestinal distress) at the rate of 500 to 800 ml/hr. The drink should be hypotonic (which means that the concentration of salts in the mixture is lower than that of salts in your

bloodstream) to aid absorption. Drink a solution containing a carbohydrate content of 2 to 7% for the first 90 minutes, 7 to 10% for the next hour, and 10 to 15% thereafter.

- The ideal sodium chloride concentration for the drink is 60 mmol/l (a measure of the osmotic strength). Because concentrations greater than 20 mmol/l are unpalatable, the remainder can be taken in the form of a 1 g sodium chloride tablet every hour.
- Experiment with eating fatty foods when you run for more than two hours. While there is as yet little scientific knowledge to confirm the benefits of this approach, there are signs that this could be helpful. The fact that some runners experience a craving for chocolate after a marathon and a revulsion for carbohydrate, is one such sign.
- Put into practice the mental imagery techniques described below (see pp. 192–4). This will become increasingly important as the race progresses, particularly after 32 km when both you and your muscle glycogen are likely to be exhausted.
- Expect to encounter 'bad patches' where you may feel like 'bailing' or quitting the race. Unless you are suffering severe diarrhoea or vomiting, experiencing light-headedness or

Running in tight groups or 'buses' makes it easier to sustain a steady pace drowsiness, or cannot rid yourself of chest pain by stopping or lying down, don't give up! The bad patches are likely to pass, and it will be difficult to overcome the sense of failure next time round. However, if you are experiencing any of the symptoms listed above, it is essential to stop immediately.

MENTAL PREPARATION

The essence of athletic competition is that success is measured according to achievement in the context of certain defined competition criteria, such as the presence of other athletes, each attempting to outrun the next. In addition, spectators are often present.

For some athletes, these criteria are unfortunate. They perform impressively in the informal context of training, but, for some reason, are unable to replicate these efforts in a race. For others, the reverse is true. They often struggle to match the efforts of their peers and team-mates in training, but on race day they are unbeatable.

Competition is all about performance under race conditions. We have discussed the role of physical preparation in racing. Just as important, but almost always underestimated, is mental preparation, and we discuss here various mental racing strategies which will help us to run our best.

Racing strategy 1: Store creative energy

Our bodies are ready. Now we must seek out the correct environment so that the final arbiter of performance – our minds – can be equally well prepared. Runners aiming for their best races must devote their time during the last week to mental preparation for the race. For the lonely long-distance runner about to face a most taxing ordeal, this, we suspect, is best done in solitude.

The first priority is to store creative energy. Running requires mental energy, and if this energy has been exhausted in other pursuits, not enough will remain for you to be completely focused on the race. If we are mentally drained through stress in our work environment, for example, we should not plan to race hard.

There are at least three ways to harness creative energy prior to the race.

- Firstly, we must reduce our training loads. This not only allows our body time to recover, but stores the mental energy normally used during training.
- Secondly, we must begin to sleep more, relax, and avoid any extra stresses, particularly at work. Although some individuals cope relatively well on sleep deprivation, this generally impairs racing performance and should be avoided.
- Thirdly, we must avoid any new creative activities at work.

Racing strategy 2: Practice mental imagery or visualization

One of the reasons for storing creative energy is to be able to 'run the race' in your mind over and over again before you run it on the road or the track.

As children, we enjoyed vivid imaginations. The world of make-believe was all-important and governed our lives to such an extent that the dividing line between reality and imagination became blurred. Sometimes what we imagined became reality. As adults, however, we have invariably fallen prey to the concrete values of materialism, and have grown accustomed to relating only to the 'real' world. We often find that we have lost the ability to enjoy play for its own sake, and our imagination has become dulled. If we wish to employ mental imagery to enhance our performances, we must strive to regain this lost dimension of our minds. We must learn from children that we too can use our imagination in such a way that the dividing line between imagination and reality becomes blurred, especially in terms of racing. One way of doing this is to practice using the 'schizophrenic technique', described in Chapter 7.

Mental imagery is a powerful tool which can be practised in a variety of contexts – during training, or while relaxing at home. It is a good idea to set aside a specific time, such as when you are in the bath, to focus your mind on specific sections of the race, your opponents, and how you might beat them. Visual material from past races, such as a video or photographs, can help to stimulate the mind to focus on the race ahead.

Mental imagery allows us to practise an activity or tactic an unlimited number of times and to review past successes and failures. We can also imagine ourselves surpassing previous performances.

You will learn the truth about your ability to cope with extreme tiredness 30 to 35 km into a marathon. Daniel Mbuli (left) and 1996 Olympic marathon gold medallist Josiah Thugwane grit their teeth 10 km from the finish of the 1993 South African marathon championships

During training, imagine yourself in a race, feeling strong and in control. Particularly when training over the race course, visualization can help to reinforce positive attitudes towards difficult sections of the race, as discussed under 'positive reinforcement' in Chapter 7.

An extension of this is to use mental imagery to visualize how to deal with dead spots (what runners call 'bad patches'), and the very real fatigue that develops during races. Dead spots occur when you lose your mental control, either because you have grown tired of concentrating on the same mental goal, or because a powerful mental distraction has suddenly appeared.

When a dead spot occurs, don't panic! Having visualized the situation prior to the race, you will be able to regain your mental control more rapidly. The best way to do this is to introduce positive self-statements, possibly through the auto-genic phrase technique. Alternatively, concentrate on the race goals you have already achieved and remind yourself of how well you are doing.

The other problem is how to cope with the very real fatigue that occurs after 32 km in the standard marathon and, to a far more debilitating degree, after 70 km in a short ultramarathon, or after 120 km in a long ultramarathon.

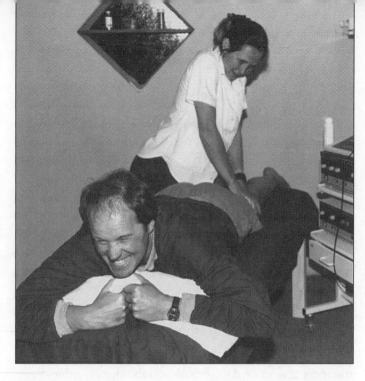

Cross-friction is a painful, although effective treatment for runners with muscle or tendon injuries. Use this experience as a rehearsal for the pain you will confront towards the end of a race, particularly the marathon

The key is to prepare mentally for when the pain will begin. During the marathon, pain begins to become a problem after about 28 km, and during the short and long ultra-marathons, after either 60 or 100 km. You should thus visualize the feelings of increased fatigue that will be experienced, and attempt to imagine how your ideal self will react positively to these challenges. One technique is to try to simulate race conditions by experiencing an external pain stimulus while visualizing your strong response to pain or fatigue at certain stages of the race. If you are receiving cross-friction physiotherapy treatment for a muscle or tendon injury, you could put the painful treatment to good use!

Another important mental tactic is to know that when the discomfort comes, it is at first worst on the uphills. Prior visualization of running these hills will have incorporated the image of recovery on the next downhill gradient. As you already know the course, you will know precisely when the next downhill section is due, and so can more easily motivate yourself to hang on just a little bit longer until you reach that section.

However, when the fatigue becomes all embracing and running downhill is just as agonizing as running uphill, then you must confront the pain, accept it, and concentrate all your efforts on not allowing it to slow you down. This is done by using techniques of segmenting and association, described below.

The last section of the race often coincides with fatigue, and we suggest that you spend time specifically visualizing this vital stage. In the example we gave in Chapter 7, of a runner being 'caught' by another athlete in the later stages of a race, we saw that it was the athlete with the stronger mind who was more likely to win. Repeatedly visualizing your performance during these vital stages will strengthen your self-concept and give you an edge over your rival.

Even if you know the course very well and have visualized yourself running it, you should still drive the course one last time, preferably the day before the race, paying special attention to the final section. As you drive the course, you should imagine once again how you will feel on the day of the race, as you run the various sections. Remind yourself of the positive self-statements that you will use as you become progressively more tired.

The primary aim of visualization is to focus your mind on the race ahead and to enable you to respond positively to race challenges. To achieve this, we should keep our focus of attention as narrow as possible, dwell on the significance of the event to us, and employ techniques to strengthen our self-concept.

Racing strategy 3: Deal with pre-race tension

We saw in Chapter 7 that there are be a range of potential psychological factors which could affect racing performance. A key factor is pre-race tension.

It has been shown that runners perform best when their levels of arousal immediately prior to competition are in mid-range. Both inadequate and excessive arousal lead to inferior performance. If you show no signs of tension, and are completely relaxed at the start, this may indicate that you are not sufficiently focused on the race, or that the race is not all that important to you. Motivation and concentration will be lacking, and your performance will suffer. Adequate physical and mental preparation for an important event should prevent this arousal deficit, which is usually a sign of disinterest.

Excessive arousal is equally destructive. If you are a 'bundle of nerves', you are also unlikely to be fully focused on

David Tsebe provides an excellent role model for associative thinking during racing

the task ahead. Apart from physical liabilities, such as an upset stomach, that could occur as a result of excessive nervousness, you will be preoccupied with self-orientation and negative thoughts, often dwelling on a minor ache, or possible equipment failure. If you are regularly troubled by this kind of malady, you should seek professional help.

Of the two situations, excessive arousal is the more common problem, and has to be controlled. There are various techniques which could be practised shortly before the start of a race to help you control your anxiety. Two of these have been described in Chapter 7, i.e. autogenic phrase training and progressive relaxation. Having become familiar with these in the months before the race, you can reap the benefits in the 24 hours prior to the start. In particular, progressive relaxation can induce sleep the night before racing, and both techniques can be profitably used at the start. Obviously, progressive relaxation will have to be adapted to fit circumstances at the start of the race – you are unlikely to be able to lie down in a darkened room!

Racing strategy 4: Don't be 'psyched out'

This phrase is often used to describe runners, usually with weak belief systems, who are unable to overcome their fears and anxieties. Through failure to adequately train the mind, these runners are often 'psyched out' of superior performances by negative thoughts.

Negative thoughts and speculations invariably increase feelings of apprehension and tension, so that once you start imagining your 'inevitable failure', doubt, fear and panic set in. These negative thoughts must be stopped and replaced by positive thoughts and self-statements and task-oriented associations. In this way, you shift your focus of attention to the positive aspects of your performance.

One helpful way to replace negative with positive thoughts is to promise yourself a reward for a certain level of performance achieved in a race. Then, rather than dropping out during an uncomfortable stretch, you can focus on the box of chocolates, ticket to a concert, day off training, overseas trip, or whatever it is that you have promised yourself. It can also help to displace negative feelings during racing if you know that someone who is important to you is watching your performance.

By training your mind through practising techniques 1 to 5 in Chapter 7, you will strengthen your self-concept and become more sensitive to your thought processes. This will enable you to become immediately conscious of negative and performance-inhibiting thoughts. The application of the autogenic phrase technique (see pp. 142–3) will then assist you in switching from a negative to positive mindset.

The worst period for negative thoughts is often at pre-race check-ins and on the start line, immediately before the start of the race. Listening to rivals describing how well they've prepared for the race, relating details of recent interval sessions, and divulging impressive target times for the race is sure to generate feelings of inadequacy or guilt about missed training sessions. Such talk is almost always wildly exaggerated, often to mask those athletes' own feelings of doubt.

Such gatherings should be avoided. As discussed above (see p. 184), once you have checked in, you should preferably isolate yourself somewhere where you can stretch, warm-up and practise the autogenic phrase technique. Better still, arrange for a friend to check in for you. One athlete who is always conspicuous by his absence during the

Big events can bring out the best or worst in athletes. Juliet Prowse is an athlete who always rises to the occasion

preliminaries of important races is Bruce Fordyce, nine times winner of the Comrades Marathon.

Racing strategy 5: Segmenting

Closely linked to the technique of using mental imagery is the idea of 'segmenting' or 'framing'. This involves mentally dividing the race into manageable portions. The trick is for you to concentrate on running the race in sections without being influenced by what still lies ahead in the race. You thus focus on holding the correct pace for the kilometre you are running, rather than concerning yourself with the many more kilometres you still need to tackle. However tired you are, you can usually imagine reaching the next marker board. This process is repeated until finally you are within striking distance of the finish. Once again, positive self-statements during this phase of the race are very helpful.

Part of segmenting is to set realistic goals for yourself, both for the entire event, and also for the intermediate segments.

For example, if you wish to run the standard 42,2 km marathon in 3:30:00, a pace of 5:00 min/km, you would set intermediate goals at 1,5,10,15,21 and 32 km of 5, 25, 50, 75, 105 and 160 minutes. Be warned that the early goals will be much easier to achieve than the latter, as you tire and find it more difficult to maintain the pace. However, armed with this knowledge, you can use the achievement of intermediate goals to stimulate yourself to keep trying.

Another useful means of segmenting the standard marathon, is to divide the race into four 10 km stretches. The final two kilometres usually present no problem for the imagination. Alternatively, you may like to tackle two 16 km segments, plus a 10 km final lap.

A final warning: the setting of intermediate goals that are unrealistically high will only serve to demotivate you once you drop behind your schedule. In addition, it is generally true that the more detailed and precise the pre-planned goals, the more pain and discomfort you will be able to endure in achieving these goals.

It is vital that you should always have a fall-back goal. For example, if it becomes apparent 20 km from the finish of the Comrades that you will be unable to complete in under 7 hours 30 minutes for a silver medal, don't just give up and start walking. Rather set a new goal, for example, making it to the finish line in under 8 hours which, in retrospect, will still be a very fine achievement.

Racing strategy 6: Association

In order to cultivate a positive and constructive mental dialogue while racing, we need to discover the specific thoughts and ideas that can spur us on. We believe that we will run our best when we concentrate very intensely and purposefully on what we are doing, thereby excluding all extraneous thoughts, including those relating to pain.

This concentration on our bodies while running is known as associative thinking, as opposed to dissociative thinking, where thoughts are directed away from the activity of running. Dr Helgo Schomer of the Department of Psychology at the University of Cape Town maintains that it is only through associative thinking that will you be able to substantially increase your aerobic conditioning while training. He also suggests that an increase in associative thinking is directly linked to an increase in training and racing intensity.

Dissociative thinking, according to Schomer, is likely to produce a less than optimum result. Only with associative thinking, which enables careful surveillance of the operation of your body, can you hope to improve your training efforts, as well as your racing performances.

Schomer concludes that if you wish to use associative thoughts optimally, you must discipline your mind to focus on the task at hand, with careful monitoring of your energy reserves and emotional state. You should also encourage and praise yourself for your efforts and calmly consider the correctness of your pace in relation to that of your opponents.

10 AFTERWORD:
Personal reflections by the authors

STEVE GRANGER

'Having had personal experience of the twin evils of the Greedy and Selfish Runner Syndromes, I believe that the key to sustainable running success lies in avoiding these maladies.

'I'm an environmental scientist by profession, and I frequently have to look at the issue of sustainability in assessing the desirability of various projects or policies. A project which looks good in the short-term, but which fails to replenish its resource base, is doomed to medium- to long-term failure. Worse still, this is usually at the expense of not only the project itself, but also the environment from which it draws its resources. Projects like these simply don't meet the criteria of sustainability, and if they're correctly assessed prior to development, they shouldn't be given the go-ahead until they've been appropriately modified.

'The parallels with running are very real to me, and I think runners should take these lessons very seriously. With hindsight, many of my efforts to run my best were counterproductive because they just weren't sustainable. I became greedy for short-term gains (and achieving some of these made me even greedier!) and didn't make adequate plans to replenish my resources. So I would embark on a rapid peaking programme, with an emphasis on quality workouts based on speed, before I had built a satisfactory endurance and strength base. I also didn't really give proper attention to recovery sessions during my programmes.

'Quite often, the result would be a few encouraging (and misleading!) race performances while I was building up to a target race. But more often than not, I'd underachieve in the race which really counted, or I'd injure myself. I hadn't grasped the basic concept of running sustainability. I think that if a coach could have assessed my training, I would have been told that my running programme – just like some of the development projects I look at in my job – wasn't sustainable, and that I should call a halt until I'd made suitable changes.

'It concerns me that many of South Africa's leading athletes seem to be on programmes that aren't sustainable, often because they have fallen prey to the Greedy Runner Syndrome. What happens is that they underperform in important championship races, become injured and demotivated, and often 'burn out' either physically or mentally. In the late 1980s, we had a lot of world-class runners in the 10 to 21 km category – people like Mathews Temane, Xolile Yawa, Zithulele Singe, David and Rami Tsebe, Matthew Motshwarateu and Lawrence Peu. But over the last two or so years, the standard for the sub-marathon distance has dropped, and I suspect that 'greedy running' might be partly to blame.

'I think that sticking to the 21 Principles of Running Your Best we describe in Chapter 4 will make it less likely that you will succumb to the Greedy Runner Syndrome. My personal advice is to remember that your training schedule is always subservient to what your body tells you (this obviously implies that you need to listen to your body). If you do this, and make sure that you incorporate adequate periods of rest and recovery into your programme, most of the remaining principles will fall into place. I think this is crucial if you want to have an enjoyable and lengthy running career.

'Finally, I'd like to say something about the second great monster, the Selfish Runner Syndrome. Obviously elite athletes (and many of them these days are professional runners) need to be totally single-minded and dedicated to the task of running their best. But for the vast majority of runners, our running careers will take second, third or fourth place behind other commitments, such as family and work. This doesn't have to diminish in any way our determination to explore the limits of our running potential, but it does suggest that the means to this end must be planned very carefully in accordance with other legitimate demands on our time and energy. I believe that if we do this creatively (along the lines sketched under Principle 20), it will lead to more harmony in our lives, and will increase our running enjoyment, longevity and ultimately success. Even full-time elite athletes need to be aware of the dangers of the Selfish Runner

Syndrome. Running may be a professional priority for them, but they also have other responsibilities and commitments – we all do. These commitments shouldn't be compromised at the expense of their general happiness; ultimately, this can only damage their running careers.'

TIM NOAKES

'It's a lucky runner who reckons that they wouldn't change anything if they had to start running all over again from scratch! Bruce Fordyce is one of the few runners I can think of who doesn't seem to have made any mistakes in his running career. I wasn't that clever, unfortunately; maybe that's why I've chosen to write about my experiences and to analyze where I went wrong.

'In retrospect, some of my mistakes were a lot more serious than others, and it's these that I would change if I could turn back the clock, and be a 20-year-old runner just starting out again.

First, I'd aim to balance the demands of long-distance running with the other demands of my life a bit more effectively. I very much doubt whether any Comrades runner has avoided making sacrifices in other facets of their lives. Running the Comrades teaches you that for each action or choice you make in life, there is an equal and opposite reaction. For every gain, no matter how beneficial it seems at the time, there is a price to pay.

'I was lucky: at least my excessive running helped in the development of my career. Perhaps this justifies the sacrifices I made at the time. But I still believe that every committed runner sooner or later has to draw up a balance sheet of the credits and debits that result from their choices.

'Maybe the real danger is to continue chasing an elusive goal for too long. Although I ran the Comrades Marathon seven times, I suspect that only four of those races were really beneficial to my growth as a person; in the other three I was going through the motions, probably too scared to let go of a lifestyle which had become so familiar. Once you have run even a single Comrades Marathon, the big problem becomes the decision about when to move on and let go of a lifestyle that has rewarded you with some of the greatest moments of your life – but which also demands that to achieve those moments, you let a whole lot of other opportunities slip by.

'So the changes I would introduce specifically to achieve a more balanced approach to running, would be to develop a long-term plan to maximize the return on the time invested in running, that planned for the day I had to start tapering off or stop. For anyone starting out running for fun, this is obviously a strange concept. Certainly it was unheard of 25 years ago, when so little was known or had been written about the sport. At that stage, the idea that one should aim to maximize the benefits of the time put into the sport would have been quite foreign. The popular idea at that time was that running was good, so more running was even better. The idea that a racing career was limited, and that one had perhaps only three fast marathons in one's legs, would have been considered ridiculous. Either you trained as hard as possible and grabbed every single opportunity to race, or you were a wimp or just lazy.

'The first key to optimizing the necessarily limited time spent in the sport is to accept one of our most important training principles: i.e. that you should aim to run as well as possible on as little training as possible (Principle 2).

'Next, I would suggest setting specific long-term goals. Perhaps the wisest option is to aim to improve your running performances slowly over many years. Performances are likely to improve for at least the first six years of a running career, with stable performances for a further 10-15 years. During the first six years, the runner should limit the number of marathons and ultramarathons that he or she runs. An absolute maximum would be two per year. The more marathons and longer races that are run in those years, the slower the best performances will be, and the shorter the competitive career. It's a much better idea to race more frequently at the shorter distances of up to 21 km. These races can be run fairly often without any apparent long-term damage. An extra bonus is that the speed gained from racing at these shorter distances improves racing performance over longer distances. Another advantage of starting with defined goals is that you can more easily recognise when those aims have been achieved, and the time to move on may have arrived.

'Another technique for getting the most out of the time spent in the activity is to set an upper limit on the amount of training you are prepared to do in terms of distance covered – 120 km a week appears to be about as much as the average competitive runner should ever aspire to. If you would like to improve your performance still further, you should increase the amount of speed training you do. I suspect that the real determinant of racing performance is more likely the amount of speed training done, rather than the total training volume, which is usually measured as the number of miles or kilometers run each week. One of the biggest mistakes that runners make is to always measure their training in terms of the volume of their training rather than in its intensity.

'Having achieved a balance in the amount of time spent training, the next balance I would try to achieve if I was a beginner runner again, would be between different sports. In particular, I'd include a significant amount of cross-training. My education in the value of cross-training started some months after finishing what would be my last Comrades Marathon in 1984. Inspired by the triathlon and even more so by the experience of managing (together with Bruce Fordyce) the South African triathlon team that won the inaugural three-day 490 km London-to-Paris triathlon, I first bought a bicycle, and then took out membership at the local gym so that I could learn to swim and perhaps complete a triathlon.

'In training for the triathlon, I learned the value and pleasure of training in three different activities. In particular, it was possible to do a great deal of exercise without feeling as weary as if the same amount of activity were done in only one sport, especially running. I also learned that cycling and swimming are sports that are very kind to the body. These activities cause fewer injuries (provided you manage to stay on board your bicycle!), and there are fewer days when you feel awful while you're training. You can usually find an activity (cycling is especially good) that can be done while recovering from a hard run or a race. The best way to recover during the first three months after the Comrades would be to cycle or swim instead of running. I learned the hard way that I wasn't able to run the Comrades each year. If I had known, I would have trained for the triathlon in the years between Comrades Marathons. I suspect that an approach like this would increase 'life expectancy' in the sport of running.

'Another advantage of doing a range of sports is that you fit your exercise to the different seasons. Cycling is ideal for autumn and spring, you can run or swim instead of cycling in the winter, and all three are suited to summer. Most of all, training in different sports allows variation, which diminishes the risk of boredom.

'I regret that my triathlon experience didn't come around sooner, as I would have liked to have competed in the Hawaiian Ironman triathlon. To have finished both the Comrades and the Ironman would, I think, be the ultimate for the amateur athlete.

'So, if I had my athletic youth again, I would definitely use the fitness and skill that I got from running to participate in a wider range of activities. This would broaden my sporting horizons, and add enjoyment to my favourite activity, running.

'When it comes to racing, here are a few last tips I wish I'd followed: I'd include more measurements to determine how fit I was at any particular stage, and to track how my fitness was improving with different training methods. Running times during training, racing over fixed distances, and simultaneously measured heart rates would be helpful. In those days, we didn't know that there was no need to run the full marathon distance to test whether or not we were in shape to run a marathon. Now we know that if you have trained for the full marathon distance, and can run 10 km in your fastest time, you are ready for your best-ever marathon.

'I also learned too late that it's essential to aim to run the second half of any distance race faster than the first. Any time gained in the first half is always lost plus at least 100% in the second half of the race.

'Finally, when running marathon and ultramarathon races I would eat and drink much more. I only realised the importance of eating or drinking a great deal of carbohydrate (especially in the last 16 km of any marathon, and in the second half of the Comrades) very late in my running career. There were many races that I would have run faster, but – even more important – would have enjoyed immeasurably more, if only I had appreciated this earlier. I still think that too few runners realise just how much easier it is to run long distances (especially the Comrades) if enough carbohydrates are consumed along the way.

'So those are the things I'd do differently if I could do it all again!'

APPENDIX 1

International Olympic Committee Medical Commission: List of doping classes and methods, 17 March 1993

Table 1

Doping classes	Doping methods	Classes of drugs subject to certain restrictions
A. Stimulants B. Narcotics C. Anabolic agents D. Diuretics E. Peptide hormones and analogues	A. Blood doping B. Pharmacological chemical and physical manipulation	A. Alcohol B. Marijuana C. Local D. Corticosteroids E. Beta-blockers

I Doping classes

A. Stimulants, e.g.

amfepramone	amfetaminil
amineptine	amiphenazole
amfetamine	benzfetamine
caffeine*	cathine
chlorphentermine	clobenzorex
chorprenaline	cocaine
cropropamide	crotetamide
dimetamfetamine	ephedrine
etafedrine	etamivan
etilamfetamine	fencamfamin
fenetylline	fenproporex
furfenorex	mefenorex
mesocarb	metamfetamine
methoxyphenamine	methylephedrine
methylphenidate	morazone
nikethamide	pemoline
pentetrazol	phendimetrazine
phenmetrazine	phentermine
phenylpropanolamine	pipradrol
prolintane	propylhexedrine
pyrovalerone	strychnine

and related compounds

* By definition, a test for caffeine is positive if the concentration in the urine exceeds 12 µg/ml. This level can be reached by drinking 3 – 5 cups of coffee in a short space of time.

Stimulants increase alertness and may reduce the sensations of fatigue. While there is some evidence that amphetamines (which are unobtainable in South Africa) may aid endurance performance by blocking the normal sensations of fatigue, and thus allowing the athlete to exceed safe levels of exhaustion, there is no scientific evidence that any other stimulants (with the exception of caffeine) aid performance in any sport. They are banned even though there is no evidence to suggest that they improve performance. It is important that athletes understand this, and do not use these agents on the false assumption that their banning means that they are aids to performance.

The majority of positive doping tests for stimulant use in South African sport are for the use of fencamfamin (found in Reactivan), and for the sympathomimetic amines, in particular ephedrine, pseudoephedrine and phenylpropanolamine. These can usually be traced back to medications used for the symptomatic treatment of colds, 'flu or hayfever, which can be bought over the counter at pharmacies without a prescription.

B. Narcotic analgesics, e.g.

alphaprodine	anileridine
buprenorphine	dextromoramide
dextropropoxyphene	diamorphine (heroin)
dihydrocodeine	dipipanone
ethoheptazine	ethylmorphine
evorphanol	methadone
morphine	nalbuphine
pentazocine	pethidine
phenazocine	tilidine
tramadol	trimeperidine

and related compounds
These agents, which reduce pain, carry a high risk of physical and psychological dependence, and are restricted in accordance with the recommendations made by the World Health Organization regarding use of narcotics.

C. Anabolic agents

1. Androgenic anabolic steroids, e.g.

androstanolone	bolasterone
boldenone	clostebol
fluoxymesterone	mesterolone
metandienone	metenolone
methyltestosterone	nandrolone
norethandrolone	oxandrolone
oxymesterone	oxymetholone
stanozolo	testosterone*

and related substances

2. Other anabolic agents, e.g.
Beta2-agonists (e.g. clenbuterol)

* Some athletes inject testosterone, the male hormone, which is normally present in the urine of males. Injection of testosterone alters the normal hormone patterns in the urine and can be detected by alterations in the concentration ratio of testosterone (T) to one of its metabolites, epitestosterone (E).

The presence of androgenic anabolic steroids in the urine indicates that the athlete has been cheating.

D. Diuretics, e.g.

acetazolamide	amiloride
bendroflumethiazide	benzthiazide
bumetanide	canrenone
chlormerodrin	chlortalidone
diclofenamine	etacrynic acid
furosemide	hydrochlorothiazide
mersalyl	spironolactone
triamterene	

and related compounds

Diuretics are misused both to reduce weight rapidly in those sports in which there are weight categories, and to reduce the concentrations of banned substances in the urine, by stimulating rapid urine excretion. This is done with the aim of avoiding detection of drug misuse.

E. Peptide hormones and analogues

chorionic gonadotrophin
corticotropin
growth hormone
erythropoietin*

* Erythropoietin, which increases the concentration of red blood cells, is used by endurance athletes to enhance performance in events lasting more than 1 - 2 minutes. At present, erythropoietin use cannot be detected, which could mean that the drug is widely abused by endurance athletes.

II Doping methods

A. Blood doping

B. Pharmacological, chemical and physical manipulation

These include techniques aimed at avoiding detection by altering the urine either chemically, pharmacologically (by taking drugs such as probenecid which delay the excretion of certain drugs), or physically (for example, by switching samples and providing drug-free urine from another person, sometimes by catheterizing the bladder of the guilty party and injecting the drug-free urine into the bladder prior to competition.)

III Classes of drugs subject to certain restrictions

A. Alcohol

Not banned

B. Marijuana

Not banned

C. Local anaesthetics

Local anaesthetics (excluding cocaine) may be used by local or intra-articular injection only when medically justified and after the authorities have been informed.

D. Corticosteroids

These are found in some asthma medications and cortizone creams. They may be used on the skin, or taken by inhalation or local intra-articular injection. Once again, the authorities must be informed when these agents are used.

E. Beta-blockers, e.g.

acebutolol   alprenolol
atenolol   labetalol
metoprolol   nadolol
oxprenolol   propranolol
sotalol

and related substances

These agents used to treat various cardiac conditions. They impair endurance performance, and hence are not restricted in those activities. However, they can improve performance in certain events which test skill, including archery, shooting, biathlon, modern pentathlon, bobsleigh, diving, and ski-jumping. Testing for these agents may thus be requested by the appropriate authorities.

APPENDIX 2

A training action plan

You might now want to put theory into action by following a training programme to achieve the goal which you have set yourself. Obviously, the best programme will be one which your coach or advisor has designed to fit your own particular requirements or 'bodyprint' (Principle 19). You may not, however, have access to such an advisor; we therefore provide five programmes of general applicability for those wishing to:

- run a 10 km race as a novice runner
- run a debut marathon as a novice runner
- run a sub-3 hour marathon
- run an elite 10 km
- run an elite marathon.

Tables 1 to 5 will enable you to follow a week-by-week schedule in order to achieve your goal, while accompanying notes briefly define and describe the various sessions (fartlek, aerobic running, tempo runs, hill striding and interval training). It is vital that you incorporate the 21 Principles for running your best into your training programme. Good luck!

Commitment to a training schedule is an important component of success in running your best. Colleen de Reuck (left), Elana Meyer and Zola Budd-Pieterse, all world-class athletes, are known for their dedication to training.

10 km debut run

Embarking on a 'running career' from a relatively sedentary lifestyle is not as straightforward as it might appear from a brief glance at Table 1 on p. 215. There are many pitfalls along the way which could cut your career short prematurely. On the positive side, we know that almost all moderately healthy people are capable of running 10 km, provided that they prepare adequately and exercise a measure of caution.

Certain sedentary people, particularly those younger than 30, could jog 5 km or even 10 km without preparation. They would almost certainly be stiff and sore for several days afterwards, but they would have achieved 'a goal'. However, problems would arise if, spurred on by this achievement, they continue their running programme on an equally ambitious footing. There is a good chance that they would break down within a few weeks, frustrated and most likely injured as well.

One extreme example of ambition in starting a running career is that of 1992 London to Brighton ultramarathon winner, Dalene Vermeulen. She was persuaded to race the tough Riebeekberg Marathon with barely a week's training behind her, and no significant prior running experience. That she finished in four hours is a tribute to her superior genetic makeup and steely determination, which enabled her to overcome the pain of a body severely overstressed during the event.

Others may scarcely be able to run 100 m before grinding to a halt and gasping for breath. To them, even the thought of running 10 km is an insurmountable obstacle. However, as in the story of the tortoise and the hare, these tortoises may be better equipped to maintain a sustainable running career lasting for weeks, months, and hopefully years, than the 'instant success' hares.

A beginner's programme must start conservatively, building a broad base of basic fitness, and taking into account some of the 'start-up' pitfalls. Because your beginner's body is unaccustomed to coping with training stress, you may find yourself tiring after some days of running, particularly if you have been too ambitious at the start. Tired muscles are less effective in acting as shock absorbers, and injuries can easily occur as a result. In addition, if you have been impatient at the start of your programme and have skipped the walking exercises, you are a probable candidate for leg injuries, either in the form of bone strain or, at worst,

Dalene Vermeulen's one-week marathon training period is not recommended! She survived thanks to mental toughness, and went on to win the London-to-Brighton marathon.

stress-fractures. These injuries typically occur six to ten weeks after the start of the programme, and are due to 'resorption' of the bone cells (a temporary weakening in the bones due to minerals in the bone cells being absorbed back into the body prior to the formation of new and stronger bone tissue). Maximal resorption typically occurs when muscle and aerobic fitness are starting to increase, thus putting the debutante runner at risk. Should the beginner translate their new sense of well-being and fitness into a more vigorous training effort, injury could well be the result.

Thus, as frustrating as it might be for some, we strongly urge all newcomers to the sport to follow an initial phase of walking. This will significantly reduce the probability of bone injury and will keep you on track for future running goals. Another way to guard against bone strain is to incorporate into your programme toe-jumping and ankle-flexing exercises to strengthen the muscles of your lower leg. These exercises are described in detail on p. 238.

Beginners' programmes often have a tendency to avoid sessions other than even-paced walking or running for a given length of time. While high-quality sessions, such as hill repetitions, are not advised at this stage, we believe that the programme can be made more interesting and effective through the incorporation of gentle speedwork. We have planned our programme accordingly, and Table 1 provides you with a 25-week schedule, geared to enable you to comfortably complete a 10 km race within that time period. The numbers refer to the time in minutes you should exercise, either through walking (W) or running (R).

The 'speed sessions' described in the key to Table 1 (A and C) should be treated with caution. The emphasis should be on fun, with the change in pace for short intervals designed to provide a stimulating diversion from constant-paced running. Faster running will also exercise certain fast twitch or white muscle fibres which may not otherwise be stressed, and will enable you to adapt more easily to longer, steady-paced running. The faster running should be done within your comfort zone and should certainly not leave you exhausted. These sessions should only be attempted once you have reached the stage in your programme where you feel comfortable with the prescribed exercise sessions. We have suggested week 15, but this could be delayed or possibly brought forward according to how you have coped with the basic programme requirements. If you would prefer to omit these sessions, simply add the total running time prescribed and treat it as a single-paced run at your accustomed pace.

Hill running, preferably off paved roads as described in the key to Table 1 (B), should also be done within your comfort level, although you could increase the work effort towards the latter stages of the programme. We do not advocate timed interval sessions or hill strides at this stage. Merely running over hilly terrain on a weekly basis will increase your power and aerobic capacity. It will also stand you in good stead should you later decide to tackle the marathon or on hill climbs during the race. Further benefits of running off-road in scenic surrounds, such as along forest trails, relate to mental refreshment. This will help you to maintain your motivation levels when your training enthusiasm wanes, which it is likely to do at some stage during your training programme. The caution discussed with respect to delaying initiating speed sessions until you feel up to them applies equally to hill running.

Another suggestion for beginners is to run in a group, or at least with another training partner committed to similar goals. Apart from the social advantages, this provides an opportunity to exchange ideas and obtain feedback on your progress. It also helps motivation when your spirit flags.

However, first check Training Tip 4 for information regarding the potential pit-falls of this suggestion.

Table 1: Training for a debut 10 km (beginners)

Day	Week 1	Week 2	Week 3	Week 4	Week 5
1	W20 mins	–	W20	W15.R5	–
2	–	W20	W20	W20	W20
3	W20	–	–	–	–
4	–	W20	W20	W20	W20
5	W20	–	W10	–	–
6	–	W20	W20	W20	W15.R15
7	W20	–	–	W10	–

Day	Week 6	Week 7	Week 8	Week 9	Week 10
1	W10	W5.R5	W5.R5	W5.R5	R10
2	W20.R5	W15.R5	W20.R5	W20.R5	W20.R10
3	–	–	–	W10.R10	–
4	W15.R5	W15.R5	W15.R5	–	W20.R10
5	–	–	–	W10.R10	–
6	W15.R5	W15.R5	W20.R5	–	W20.R10
7	–	–	–	W15.R10	–

Day	Week 11	Week 12	Week 13	Week 14	Week 15
1	W15.R5	W10.R10	W10.R10	W10.R10	W5.R15
2	W20.R10	W15.R15	W10.R20	W10.R20	W5.R25
3	–	–	–	–	–
4	W20.R10	W20.R10	W15.R15	W10.R20	W10.R15.A.R5
5	–	–	–	R10.W10	W5.R25
6	W20.R10	W15.R15	W10.R20	W10.R20	–
7	–	–	–	–	W10.R10

Day	Week 16	Week 17	Week 18	Week 19	Week 20
1	W5.R25	R30	R30	R30	–
2	–	–	–	–	R30
3	R30.B	R15.A.R10	R30.B	R30	R20
4	W5.R15	R20	R20	R30	–
5	R30	R30	–	–	R30
6	–	–	R30	R20	R30
7	W5.R15	R20	R20	R20	R15

Day	Week 21	Week 22	Week 23	Week 24	Week 25
1	–	–	–	–	R40
2	R15.A.R10	R25	R35	R20	R20
3	R30	R40	R30	–	–
4	–	–	–	R20	R20
5	R35	R30.B	R25.B	R20.C.R15	R20
6	R25	R25	R35	R15	–
7	R20	R20	R20	R20	10 km race

Key to symbols:

W = Walk, **R** = Run

A: Jog 1 min, fast 30 sec, jog 1 min, fast 30 sec, jog 30 sec, fast 30 sec, jog 1 min.

B: Complete session off-road on hilly terrain

C: Jog 2 min, fast 1 min, jog 1 min, fast 30 sec, jog 1 min, fast 30 sec, jog 1 min, fast 1 min, jog 2 min

Debut marathon

While 42 km may appear to be further from 10 km than the latter is from zero, with respect to beginners, this is not true in practice. Once again, we should stress the necessity of spending patient weeks at the start of any running pro-gramme in order to avoid injury. Once 10 km has been achieved after a 25-week programme, the groundwork has been done, and a marathon, according to our schedule in Table 2, is just another 11 weeks away.

During this time the emphasis is on adapting to a steadily increasing workload in terms of total running time. Weekly increases of between 10% and 30% are indicated, peaking at seven and a half hours of running (approximately 60 km to 80 km, depending on running speed) during the 33rd week.

If time allows, a more gradual build-up during this period is preferable, with a maximum weekly increase in distance of about 10% being advisable. Additional weeks could be fitted in between weeks 26 and 27, 27 and 28 and 32 and 33.

You should continue the variations in training suggested in the 10 km programme, i.e. the cautious use of speed and hill running, as long as you feel able to cope with these ses-sions with relative comfort. These suggestions are outlined in Table 2.

Apart from the physical training load, the mental aspects of running are also important as you approach the challenge of the marathon. Principles 13 and 17 in Chapter 4 and the whole of Chapter 7 are important reading in this respect.

Table 2: Training for a debut marathon (beginners)

As for 10 km programme (above) up to week 24. Then as follows:

Day	Week 25	Week 26	Week 27	Week 28	Week 29	Week 30
1	R40	R45	R30	R30	R35	R35
2	R20	R30	R45	R55	R60	R70
3	–	–	R30	R30.B	R35.B	R10.C.R15
4	R20	R10.C.R10	R50	R55	R60	R70
5	R50	R50	–	–	R35	R35
6	–	R45	R60	R80	R90	R100
7	R30	–	–	–	–	–

Day	Week 31	Week 32	Week 33	Week 34	Week 35	Week 36
1	R40	R40	R40	R40	R40	R40
2	R80	R90	R90	R90	R90	R20
3	R15.C.R15	R40.B	R40.B	R15.C.R15	R20.R.R15	R30
4	R40	R90	R90	R90	R30	–
5	R35	R40	R40	R40	R40	–
6	R110	R120	R150	R100	R80	–
7	–	–	–	–	R20	Marathon

Key to symbols:
W = Walk, **R** = Run
A: Jog 1 min, fast 30 sec, jog 1 min, fast 30 sec, jog 30 sec, fast 30 sec, jog 1 min.
B: Complete session off-road on hilly terrain
C: Jog 2 min, fast 1 min, jog 1 min, fast 30 sec, jog 1 min, fast 30 sec, jog 1 min, fast 1 min, jog 2 min

Elite 10 km to half Marathon

The programme in Table 3 can be followed for any sub-marathon distance, although it could be adapted by increasing training distances when preparing for longer races, should you wish to do so.

The programme has been planned to emphasise three different facets or phases of preparation as you continue through your 13-week schedule. These are training for endurance, power and speed. Although the daily training schedules focus primarily on the achievement of each of these qualities in turn (this is why hill training is emphasised during the second phase and track work during the last), the phases are not exclusive. Each phase, while emphasising a particular facet, involves training for all three qualities: endurance, power and speed.

It is assumed that you will have undertaken adequate base training prior to beginning the peaking programme. Ideally, we recommend at least four months of base training along similar lines to those indicated in Table 3. After a recovery week, during which your level of fitness should be evaluated, you can commence the peaking programme.

Trhoughout this programme, it is essential to remember Principle 4 – your training schedule is subservient to what your body tells you. This applies both to the volume of training and its intensity. If, for example, you are scheduled to run 12 km at a sustained pace and feel exhausted before you start, either abort the session completely, or jog at a relaxed pace for 5 km only.

It should be stressed that each session indicated in Tables 3 to 5, with the exception of easy-paced aerobic runs, should be preceded by a warm-up jog of about 10 to 15 minutes at a comfortable pace, and should be completed with a similar cool-down jog of between 5 and 10 minutes. In addition, supplementary exercises described below (pp. 228 – 238) should be carried out before or after the sessions, or both. It is especially important to carry out basic stretching exercises (described on pp. 229 – 230) before a training session, preferably after the warm-up run.

Remember that your recovery days are crucial for success in attempting to run your best. If you have not sufficiently recovered from a previous work-out, there is little point in undertaking another. Be flexible and respond to your body's demands. Remember Bruce Fordyce's dictum: 'When in doubt, rest!'

Table 3: Training for a 10 km race (elite athletes)

PHASE	WEEK	M	T	W	T	F	S	S
BASE TRAINING	as long as possible	8	12–17s	6–8e	10–15e	(5)	5–15h	18–25e
REST/ EVALUATION	0	F1	5–8e	5TT	5–8e	5;S1	5–10h	5–8e
START PEAKING PROGRAMME								
ENDURANCE	1	F2*	10–12e*	M1	H2*	5–8e;S2	10–15h	L2
	2	F3	8–10e*	M2	H1*	5e;S1	3x3h	L1
	3	F2*	10–12e*	M1	H2*	5–8e;S2*	10–15h	L3
REST/ EVALUATION	4	F1	5–8e	2TT	5–8e	5;S1	10–29h	L1
POWER	5	F4*	H2*	5TT	H5*	5–8;S2*	T1	L2
	6	F5	H1*	10e	H6*	5e;S1	5TT	L1
	7	F4*	H2*	125*	H5*	8–10e;S2*	T1	L3
REST/ EVALUATION	8	F1	5–8e	2TT	5–8e	5e;S1	10TT	L1
SPEED	9	F4*	10–12s*	T6	H3*	5–8e;S2*	T8	L3
	10	F5*	8–10e*	T5	H1*	5e;S1	5TT	L1
	11	F4*	10–12e*	T6	H3*	5–8e;S2	T8	L3
TAPER	12	F1	5–8s	3TT	5–8e	5–8e;S2	P1	10e
	13	P1	P2	P3	P4	P5	RACE	

Key to symbols

* = include a second training session (probably in the morning) on these days by running 5 to 10 km at easy pace. Alternately, cross-train for 30 to 60 minutes (swim, cycle, gym work-out, etc.), should leg tiredness dictate this

e = easy pace: about 30% slower than your best time for the distance

s = sustained pace: about 15% slower than your best time for the distance
h = hard pace: about 5 - 10% slower than your best time for the distance.
Number followed by lower case letter = distance in km at specified pace (e.g. 10-12e = 10 to 12 km at easy pace)
Upper case letter followed by number = codes explained below
Number followed by TT = time trial at specified distance in km

F FARTLEK

Fartlek is a Swedish word meaning speed-play and consists of a combination of slow and fast running over a variety of surfaces and terrain. Fartlek is a cornerstone of our training schedule. While it can be used as an unstructured session of spontaneous bursts of speed for fun at random intervals in scenic surrounds (and this is how we have used it during each recovery week), the more serious and structured sessions of fartlek will significantly increase your aerobic power and speed endurance. The speed bursts should represent between 80 to 90% effort for the distance and you should always feel in control.

F1 Informal (unstructured) fartlek: random bursts of speed of between 15 to 45 seconds, separated by jogging intervals lasting 60 to 120 seconds. Emphasis is on play. The session should last about 20 to 30 minutes, and its aim is to aid physical and mental recovery. It is also useful for sharpening during the pre-race taper.

F2 Four to five repetitions of 3 minutes each, separated by 90 second jogging intervals.

F3 Staggered formation fartlek: hard running of consecutive intervals of 1, 2, 3, 3, 2, 1 minutes separated by jogging periods of 60 seconds (following the 1 and 2 minute intervals) and 90 seconds (following the 3 minute intervals). Stronger athletes can add another session of 1, 2, 2, 1 minute bursts separated by 60 second jogging periods.

F4 Tapered fartlek: 3 intervals of hard running for 5 minutes each, separated by 90 second jogging intervals; jog 3 minutes; 3 hard-running intervals of 3 minutes each, separated by 60 second jogs; jog 3 minutes; 3 bursts of 30 seconds each, separated by 30 second jogs.

F5 Staggered formation fartlek: hard running during consecutive intervals of 1, 2, 3, 2, 1, 1, 2, 3, 2, 1 minutes, each separated by 60 seconds jogging; jog 3 minutes; strong bursts of consecutive intervals of 15, 30, 45, 30, 15 seconds separated by 30 second jogging intervals.

M MIDDLE DISTANCE RUNNING
M1 Tough tempo: 10 km easy; 5 km firm (5 - 10 sec per km slower than 10 km race pace); 5 km easy. The faster 5 km stretch should be done on relatively flat, smooth terrain. The idea is to try to run hard, but in a relaxed manner in order to adapt the body into 'cruising' at higher speeds.

M2 15 km easy

TT TIME TRIAL OR TEMPO RUN
This should be carried out at about 85% effort, or equivalent to 10 km race pace for 3 km and 5 km time trials. Run over a smooth surface on flat terrain. Try to run in as relaxed a manner as possible, even at faster pace. Precede and conclude the session with a 15 minute jog. Speed of recovery of heart rate is the important monitoring factor in time trials. Faster pulse recovery for equivalent effort in successive time trials, or faster times for equivalent pulse recovery are the determinants of success, rather than simply aiming at faster running times.

T TRACK WORK (Interval training)
Speed work is essential for athletes seeking to run their best, and track training is the most basic form of speed exercise. Controlled running at speed over shorter measured distances will lead to faster times over 10 km and the marathon.

Most track training takes place over measured intervals. We have included in these schedules a balance between training over fewer, longer (extensive) intervals, and running a larger number of shorter intervals at faster speed, with shorter recovery periods. In general, the emphasis for distance runners should be on high intensity aerobic running, rather than on 'anaerobic' sprinting. All track sessions should be preceded and concluded with 15 to 20 minutes of easy-paced running.

T1 Four intervals of 1 000 m at 10 seconds per km faster than your best 10 km pace, each separated by 90 seconds jogging. For example, if your best 10 km time is 40 minutes, complete these intervals in 3:50 per interval.

T2 Four intervals of 1 600 m at 5 seconds per km faster than your best 10 km pace, each separated by 90 seconds jogging. For example, if your best 10 km time is 30 minutes, complete these intervals in 4:43 per interval.

T3 Three intervals of 1 600 m at 5 seconds per km faster than 10 km pace, each separated by 90 seconds jogging.

T4 Four intervals of 1 000 m at 20 seconds per km faster than 10 km pace, each separated by 5 minutes jogging. For example, if your best 10 km time is 40 minutes, complete these intervals in 3:40 per interval.

T5 Four intervals of 1 600 m at 20 seconds per km faster than 10 km pace, each separated by 5 minutes jogging. For example, if your best 10 km time is 30 minutes, complete these intervals in 4:28 per interval.

T6 Two intervals of 800 m; 8 intervals of 400 m; 5 intervals of 200 m at 5 seconds, 15 seconds and 40 seconds respectively per km faster than 10 km pace; each interval separated by 90 seconds jogging; each set separated by 5 minutes jogging. For example, if your best 10 km time is 40 minutes, complete these intervals in 3:08, 1:30 and 40 seconds respectively per interval.

T7 Eight intervals of 400 m; 5 intervals of 200 m at 15 seconds and 40 seconds respectively per km faster than 10 km pace; each interval separated by 90 seconds jogging; each set separated by 5 minutes jogging.

T8 One interval of 1 600 m; 2 intervals of 800 m; 8 intervals of 400 m at 5 seconds, 10 seconds and 15 seconds respectively faster than 10 km pace; each interval separated by 90 seconds jogging; each set separated by 5 minutes jogging. For example, if your best 10 km time is 30 minutes, complete these intervals in 4:43, 2:16 and 1:06 respectively per interval.

S STRIDES
These are series of short distance long-stride sprints which are used as looseners prior to racing or for sharpening.

S1 Six to ten sprints of 40 m to 50 m with jogging for equivalent distance in between.

S2 Six to ten sprints of 100 m with jogging for equivalent distance in between.

H HILL RUNNING
Running on hills builds muscle power and aerobic efficiency and this is an important dimension in training to run your best. While some weight training is recommended to develop specific upper body strength, incorporating hill sessions into your training schedules will develop lower-leg strength, muscle power and fitness. Especially if time limitations prevent you from tackling various cross-training programmes (such as weights, swimming or cycling) in order to develop an all-round fitness, hill training is vital if you are to realise your potential as a runner. We describe several hill training sessions to assist you in achieving your goal. The usual warm-ups and cool downs should be included for the last two hill exercises.

H1 Run on hills for 40 minutes.

H2 Run on hills for 40 minutes, working harder on the inclines.

H3 Run on hills for 60 minutes.

H4 Run on hills for 60 minutes, working harder on the inclines.

H5 Run up a slope for 3 minutes at sustained pace; jog down; repeat 4 times (total of 5 repetitions); jog 5 minutes; run up a slope (preferably steeper than the original) for 200 m at fast pace; jog down; repeat 4 times; jog 5 minutes; run down a gentle slope for 150 m at fast pace; jog up; repeat 4 times.

H6 Run up a slope for 90 seconds at hard pace; jog down; repeat 4 times; run up a steeper slope for 150 m (at faster pace); jog down; repeat 4 times.

L LONG RUNS

The long training run, usually undertaken over the week-end, is often the focus of an athlete's training programme (and social life!) From both a mental and physical perspective, it is essential that your schedule includes regular aerobic runs of between 15 km and 32 km. Especially if you are to run a marathon, it is important to have run about 65% to 75% of your race distance in training on several occasions. Even if you are training for sub-marathon distances, it is important that you include regular longer runs in your race build-up, in order to develop muscle endurance.

L1 Long aerobic running: 15 - 18 km

L2 Long aerobic running: 18 - 22 km

L3 Long aerobic running: 22 - 25 km

L4 Long aerobic running: 25 - 32 km

P TAPER

We have discussed the importance of tapering prior to a race in Chapters 4 and 9. Essentially, tapering involves a gradual reduction of your work load in training prior to your race. We believe that an intensive taper, in which total training volume (rather than speed) is reduced prior to racing will produce the most satisfactory results.

P1 Run 5 intervals of 1000 m at 15 to 20 seconds per km faster than your best 10 km pace; jog 90 seconds between each interval; 10 minutes warm-up and cool-down. If your best 10 km time is 40 minutes, complete these intervals in 3:40 to 3:45 per interval.

P2 Run 4 intervals as described above.

P3 Run 3 intervals as described above.

P4 Run 2 intervals as described above.

P5 Run 1 interval as described above.

Elite marathon

Our programme for an elite marathon is similar to that for an elite 10 km and is also designed to follow three specific phases: training for endurance, power and speed. These are the essentials in any programme of distance running. The distance you race will determine the mix of the ingredients. Thus for the marathon, there is a greater emphasis on training volume, although speed work is not neglected.

Our introductory comments on the elite 10 km programme should also be read in conjunction with this programme. We stress again the importance of mental training for the marathon. Just as you set aside time to complete the physical components of this schedule, you should also make time to prepare your mind for the race. We discuss this more fully in Chapters 7 and 9.

As your training volume increases, proper rest and recovery sessions become even more important. You may be able to perform close to your best in a slightly undertrained condition, but you will be way off your target time if you have overtrained in any way.

Notes

Table 4: Training for the marathon (elite athletes)

PHASE	WEEK	M	T	W	T	F	S	S
BASE TRAINING	as long as possible	8	12–17s	6–8e	10–15e	(s)	5–15h	18–25e
REST/ EVALUATION	0	F1	5–8e	5TT	5–8e	5;S1	5–10h	5–8e
START PEAKING PROGRAMME								
ENDURANCE	1	F2*	12–15e*	M1	H4*	5–8e;S2	10–15h	L3
	2	F3	10–12e*	M2	H3*	5e;S1	3x3h	L2
	3	F2*	12–15e*	M1	H4*	5–8e;S2*	10–15h	L4
REST/ EVALUATION	4	F1	5–8e	5TT	5–8e	5;S1	10–20h	L2
POWER	5	F4*	H4*	5TT	H5*	5–8;S2*	T2	L3
	6	F5	H3*	15e	H6*	53;S1	5TT	L2
	7	F4*	H4*	18e*	H5*	8–10;S2*	T2	L4
REST/ EVALUATION	8	F1	5–8e	2TT	5–8e	5;S1	20–30TT	L2
SPEED	9	F4*	12–15s*	T6	H3*	5–8e;S2*	5TT	L4
	10	F5*	10–12e*	T4	H3*	53;S1	T8	L2
	11	F4*	12–15e*	T6	H3*	5–8e;S2	5TT	L4
TAPER	12	F1	8–10e	T4	H1	5–8e;S2	T7	L2
	13	1	10s	3TT	15e	5–8e;S2	P1	15e
	14	P2	P3	P4	P5	RACE		

The key to these symbols is on pages 219 to 224

Sub-3 hour marathon

This programme has been designed as much for those who, through other commitments and responsibilities, are unable to take the time needed to complete the schedule described under Table 4 as for those who may lack the ability to run an 'elite' marathon. While this programme has been designed on the same principles as the one for elite athletes, there is less emphasis on speed work (your natural speed is unlikely to be a barrier to running at slower than 4 minutes per km). In addition, the volume of training has been reduced. This can, of course, be adjusted to suit your individual requirements.

Notes

Table 5: Training for the marathon (sub-three hours)

PHASE	WEEK	M	T	W	T	F	S	S
BASE TRAINING	as long as possible	8	10–15s	5–8e	8–10e	–	5–10h	15–20e
REST/ EVALUATION	0	F1	5e	5TT	5e	–	5e	10e
START PEAKING PROGRAMME								
ENDURANCE	1	F2	(5–8e)	M2	H1	–	10–15h	L2
	2	F3	(5–8)	M2	H1	–	3x3h	L1
	3	F2	(5–8)	M1	H3	–	10–15h	L3
REST/ EVALUATION	4	F1	(5)	5TT	5e	–	race 15	L1
POWER	5	F2	(5–8e)	H4	15s	–	3x3h	L2
	6	F3	(5e)	H6	10s	–	4x1h	L1
	7	F5	(5–8e)	H5	15s	–	3x3h	L3
REST/ EVALUATION	8	F1	(5)	3TT	5e	–	race 21	L1
SPEED	9	F2	(5–8e)	T7	15s	–	T3	L3
	10	F5	(5–8e)	T7	10s	–	T3	L2
TAPER	11	F1	(5–8e)	3TT	8e	–	2x3h	15e
	12	F1	10e	5e	5e	–	RACE	

Supplementary exercises

Stretching

Distance running can lead to tightening of the muscles and reduced flexibility. A disciplined stretching programme can ensure that these adverse effects are minimized. Other benefits of stretching include reduced risk of injury, reduced muscle soreness after strenuous exercise, and improved athletic performance.

Static stretching, where the stretch position is assumed and held for 30 to 60 seconds, is the most effective form of stretching as it minimises muscle tension build-up.

A comprehensive stretching programme can be found in *Lore of Running* or *Running Injuries*. Here we illustrate four important stretches which should be regarded as the basic minimum. Recent research has queried the advisability of stretching 'cold' muscles before exercising. It may thus be wise to stretch after your session, or after a 10-minute warm-up before training.

Lower leg exercises

Do the following exercises two to three times a week, preferably before a training session. They should be done in running shoes on a firm surface which offers some cushioning, for example, a grass track or the aerobics floor. Do not perform on concrete.

1. Hop on your toes for 30 second periods at different speeds. As you become more proficient, try flexing your ankles by pulling your toes towards your shins and then do the hopping on one leg at a time. Do four to six sets per session with equivalent rest periods between each set.

2. Walk on your heels for 20 m to 30 m. Do three sets with equivalent rest periods.

3. Walk on your toes in the following sequence: 20 m to 30 m in a straight line; 20 m to 30 m with your hips rotated inward (pigeon-toed); 20 m to 30 m with your hips rotated outwards (duck-feet). Do three sets with 30 seconds rest between sets.

4. Do ankle flex repetitions by leaning against a wall, your heels about 300 mm from the wall. Raise your toes as high as possible towards your shins and lower your feet until just above the ground. Do 20 repetitions and two to three sets with 30 seconds rest between sets. As you become more proficient, carry out this exercise on one foot at a time.

1. Lower leg

Lean against a wall with your back foot flat and your head up. Slowly bend your arms and lower your body towards the wall. First do the exercise with a straightened leg to stretch the outside calf muscle (the gastrocnemius), and then with the leg bent to stretch the inner calf muscle (the soleus).

2. Hamstrings

Although runners tend to do hamstring stretches by raising one leg against a support, this carries a risk of injury and also puts strain on the lower back. You could reduce this risk by by sitting with one leg stretched out (as shown) and grasping your ankle. Now lean gradually towards that foot, keeping your back straight.

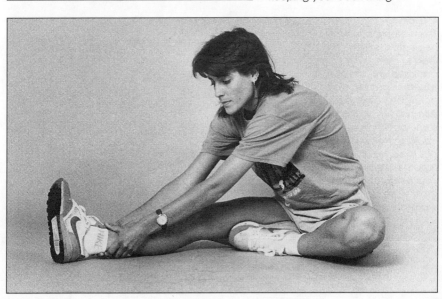

3. Quadriceps

Grasp your foot with your hand and gently pull towards your buttocks. There are various forms of this stretch, but the one illustrated gives maximal stretch. It is not recommended for those who have knee injuries.

4. Groin

This stretch is often neglected, which can lead to injury. With your back straight and feet together, push down gently on your knees. Alternatively, in the same position, you could grasp your toes, pull the soles of your feet together, and then pull your heels towards your groin while leaning forward

Big 6

Distance running produces strong back and hamstring muscles, but leaves the abdominals and upper body relatively weak. This muscle imbalance can cause a 'bow-string effect' in the back, leading to lower back pain. South African distance running coach Bobby McGee recommends the following exercises to build stomach muscles and upper body strength, which, together with appropriate stretching, will help to correct this imbalance. Do the exercises two to three times per week after training sessions, but stop five days before a major race. Initially do one set of seven to fifteen repetitions of each exercise, and gradually build up to three sets of each. Because eccentric muscle contractions play a crucial role in muscle development, the return or lowering phase of each exercise is as important as the lifting phase. Lower yourself slowly, with control, and avoid building up a rhythm. Concentrate on completing each exercise as an individual unit.

Coach Bobby McGee supervises elite runner Juliet Prowse as she begins the 'Big 6'

1. Abdominal curls

Lie on your back with arms outstretched behind your head. You may find it helps to grasp a support. Bend your knees, while keeping your back flat and unarched (1a). Draw your knees towards your chin (1b) and return to your original position without allowing your feet to touch the ground. You might like to place your feet against a wall during this exercise, but be careful to use the wall as a support only, not as a springboard to launch the next curl, or as a resting place. Once you become proficient, you should abandon the hand support and the wall.

2. Dips
Sit against a solid object or step 500 mm - 700 mm in height. Flex your arms about 80° - 90° behind you, with your hands resting on top of the step (2a). Raise yourself by straightening your arms, minimising hip movement as you do so (2b).

3. Half-jacks

Lie on your flattened back with your legs raised, about 20° above vertical. In order to prevent your back arching, you may find it helpful at first to put your feet against a wall. Place your hands on the ground on either side of your hips (3a), then curl up by stretching your hands along the ground and lifting shoulders (3b).

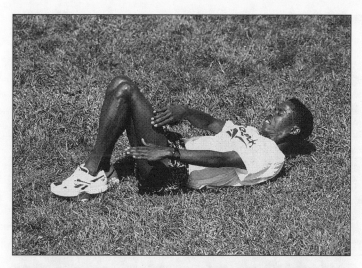

4. Sidewinders

Lie flat on your back with your knees bent. Place your left foot on top of your right to minimise use of quadriceps (4a). Raise your right shoulder with a twisting movement and lift your upper back, moving both arms forward on the left side of your left leg (4b). Try to contract one side of your stomach by pushing the base of your rib cage towards your pelvis. Lower yourself, but do not allow your left shoulder to touch the ground. Repeat the exercise, but this time raise your left shoulder in order to use the other side of your body. During this exercise, your spine should be tilted down to one side.

5. Push-ups
The hands should be comfortably placed slighter wider apart than the shoulders (5a). Lower your body until just above the floor or ground and raise again. Initially you may do knee push-ups (5b) before gaining strength. The back should be flat or rounded, not arched.

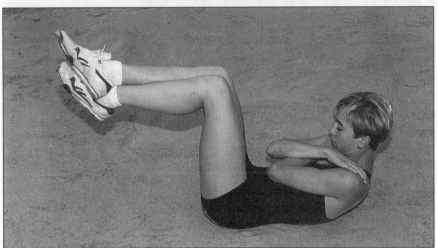

6. Crunches

Lie on your back with your knees raised above the ground, and your hips and knees bent at 90°. Cross one foot over the other (6a). Curl up by lifting your shoulders, but do not lift your lower back (6b). Lower down slowly. Your elbows should be flat against your chest during the exercise.

APPENDIX 3

Suggested chart for goal-setting (to be used in conjunction with your log book)

YEAR ....

1. Target priority races for the year:

Race	Opponent to beat	Time target	Time actual	Position
....	....	....	....	....
....	....	....	....	....
....	....	....	....	....
....	....	....	....	....

2. Target training programme (average values):

	days per week	km per month	act. days	act. km
Jan – Mar	....	....	....	....
Apr – Jun	....	....	....	....
Jul – Sept	....	....	....	....
Oct – Dec	....	....	....	....

Planned hard training months ....
Planned easy training months ....
Planned rest months ....

3. Target achievements for the year:

Write down non-time targets for your running year. Include items such as team selection, medals, titles, opponents to beat, sponsorship, enjoyment, injuries rehabilitated, running partners, balance with other facets of life, etc.

....
....
....
....
....
....
....
....
....

4. Target times (T = target; A = actual)

ROAD

Distance	PB All time (h:m:s)	PB 1995	PB 1996	PB Jan-Jul 1997		PB Aug-Dec 1997		PB Jan-Jul 1998		PB Aug-Dec 1998		PB Jan-Jul 1999		PB Aug-Dec 1999	
				TARGET	ACTUAL	TARGET	ACTUAL	TARGET	ACTUAL	TARGET	ACTUAL	TARGET	ACTUAL	TARGET	ACTUAL
10 km															
15 km															
21,1 km															
42,2 km															
56 km															
Comrades															

4. Target times (T = target; A = actual)

TRACK

Distance	PB All time (m:s)	PB 1995	PB 1996	PB Jan-Jul 1997		PB Aug-Dec 1997		PB Jan-Jul 1998		PB Aug-Dec 1998		PB Jan-Jul 1999		PB Aug-Dec 1999	
				TARGET	ACTUAL	TARGET	ACTUAL	TARGET	ACTUAL	TARGET	ACTUAL	TARGET	ACTUAL	TARGET	ACTUAL
100 m h															
100 m h															
110 m															
200 m															
400 m h															
400 m															
800 m															
1 500 m															
3 000 m															
3 000 m h															
5 000 m															
10 000m															